MANHASSET STORIES:
More Baby Boomer Memories

Suzanne McLain Rosenwasser

Manhasset Times
Media Group, LLC
2012

Printed in the United States of America.

For further information, or signed copies, contact:
Manhasset Times Media Group,LLC,
at suzannerosenwasser@gmail.com

The *Manhasset Stories* series is available in paperback at The Little Shop around the Corner in Manhasset, The Dolphin Bookstore in Port Washington New York, and from online booksellers (also in ebook format).

ISBN: 978-0-615-71918-4
Library of Congress (PCN): 2012921340

Cover Photo: Michael A. Rosenwasser
Vintage 1957 Chevrolet Bel Air available at Chevrolet Car Company. Roswell GA. http://www.californiacarco.com
Author Photo: Christopher McLain
Proofreader: MTMG

For my Sister:
Mary McLain Smith
1945-2003

I carry your heart with me
-ee cummings

TABLE OF CONTENTS:

Thoughts and Prayers

Hurricane Sandy tore into New York's metropolitan area on October 29, 2012, just as this book was headed to press.

The residents of Manhasset were plunged into darkness and cold with millions of other people on the East Coast. Many Manhasset homes suffered irreparable damage when dozens of those beloved, ancient hardwoods we all admire, couldn't hold themselves up any longer.

No physical damage has been reported, but emotional scars have deeply wounded so many of our Baby Boomers and the people they love. Many have sustained incredible losses.

Clean-up and recovery will be long and difficult. If you have friends affected anywhere - in any place this storm hit - go out of your way for them; if you don't, go out of the way for the friends you haven't met yet.

~ SMR

PREFACE
You Can Go Home Again

The response I received to the first book of Manhasset stories overwhelmed me. I was embraced by childhood friends through emails and phone calls, as well as in person at the Manhasset Library in May 2012.

I received endearing notes from Manhasset people I hadn't known before, but who are very much a part of my Manhasset world now. I also heard from people who grew up in towns like Manhasset, Baby Boomers themselves, being raised in the new American suburbs of post-WWII. One was my college friend Jane from Garden City, who said she and her relatives read the book and thought it could have been their hometown during the same era.

The Manhasset messages travelled like this.

Gus, from my Kindergarten class, not only came to hear me speak at Hofstra University, but also his Manhasset wife, Joan, turned out to be best friends with my K-12 classmate, Ruth, who sent me a message about the first kiss she got in an SMS cloak room.

The next thing I knew Roger, from my elementary school, bus stop on Chapel Road - and friends with the aforementioned Gus - dropped me a kind reminiscence and, in an extraordinary gesture, found Sr. Louisa from the "Queen Mary" story. She is Sister Theresa McElroy now and just recently retired from years of service. She resides at Our Lady of Peace in Scranton, PA and would love to hear from you. We spoke on the phone. I must admit, I felt eight years old again.

Not long after that, I heard from Maury because he knows Sue Ellen who crowned the St. Mary's Queen of May in 1956. Maury, who is now a Monsignor in Texas, sent copies of the book to all sorts of Manhasset friends.

Maury found out about the first book of Manhasset stories from Jerry who was a boyfriend of mine in high school.

Jerry, who has the longest email list of Manhasset Baby Boomers you'd ever want to see, sent out the word that the book was a fun read.

Sales peaked. No kidding.

Then Pat, the oldest sister of my forever friend, Terry - Most Humorous, SMS Class of 65 - called to laugh and cry about so many wonderful days we shared in their home on Hunt Lane. Terry isn't alive any more to tell us her stories, but she is definitely in the Manhasset Storytellers Hall of Fame.

I also heard from Karen and Kathy, childhood friends whose parents were my parents' friends. These are the kids I swam with in the summer time. When our parents were visiting, we chased after lightning bugs on Eakins Road or ate endless Good Humors' from an Elderfields' Road freezer.

Then there was the Circle gang - MJ, Debbie, Kathie, Maureen - geez, too many of them to name, but their story is told in this book.

Ralph, who climbed trees with me when we were eight, dropped me a line, as did Johnny, who said he felt like we were all together being kids again when he was reading. Ray and I connected on Facebook over a short span of high school time when we all hung out with the same people.

Betty - who turned out to be the sister of John, Valedictorian of my 1965 high school class - said Manhasset Stories made her homesick enough to throw an "I Grew Up in Manhasset Reunion," (now held annually each September at Edison's - come one, come all).

I got a note from Didi - formerly of Inness Place - who chatted about the book with Georgette - owner of the actual Tender Bar - both of whom were visiting their moms at the Sands Point Rehabilitation Center.

Didi and I worked at Jaffee's Department Store with Peggy, who wrote to say how well she remembered the Jaffee days after reading the story about working there in the 60s.

Peggy's sister-in-law, Carol, is married to Peggy's brother, Joe. Carol came to the Manhasset Public Library to share Manhasset stories with Wendy, Judy, and Mary (aka the "Birthday Girls") - all from St. Mary's. Mary told a story about my sister being called to the office in high school after experiencing some kind of "altercation" at Town Hall Pharmacy. I never knew my sister to be in trouble, and I - who logged many an hour in the Principal's Office - took some vicarious pleasure in hearing of this transgression 50 years later.

However, one of my favorite moments was person to person.

When I spoke at the Manhasset library, I asked the audience to share their Manhasset stories. A gentleman stood and said:

"I'm Bob Peck, I'm sure no one knows me...."
Disclaimers from the audience came all at once:
"Sure we know you!"
"You're Elizabeth's brother..."
"You lived on Beechwood, right?"
"Didn't you work at the Post office for awhile?"
There's no getting away from Baby Boomer Manhasset.

The Peck family moved to their Beechwood Avenue home in 1943 from Minnesota where Bob's dad worked for CBS Radio. Upon receiving his promotion to the New York station, Mr. Peck followed the advice of his colleagues, including Walter Cronkite: "The only place to live is Manhasset." Bob's been a resident ever since.

That day I heard stories about Nancy's family moving to Manhasset for the schools in 1952, and Mary's family choosing Manhasset when the Throgs Neck Bridge declared eminent domain on their Bayside home in 1958.

Phyllis told a story about her family buying the only house in their price range at the bottom of Longridge Road. One day in the 60s, a garbage truck lost its brakes and crashed through it when no one was home.

Cara's parents from the Bronx fell in love on the LIRR, married, and moved to Garden Turn in the late 30s. Mark's mother, in the 1960s, fell in love with a barn-red house surrounded by a white picket fence and a slew of neighborhood kids in Gull's Cove. Robert's family came in 1930 because Manhasset residents didn't have to change trains at Jamaica on the way into the city.

Whatever the reasons our parents made Manhasset our home, they gave us a gift that has never left us. The experience was so rich and vivid, we can call it back at the drop of a hat with another Manhasset story.

So with that in mind, here are a few more.

Suzanne McLain Rosenwasser
November 2012

The Park Avenue Canopy

All my return journeys to Manhasset begin at the sycamore trees.

I enter Park Avenue from Port Washington Boulevard by habit and slowly follow the sycamores to Plandome Road.

The graceful arch of the trees allows my vision to tunnel, framing a street that has kept its character ever since it first came into my view in the early 1950s.

The trees, also known as American Planes, had been there way before my family came along in 1951, of course, and most Manhasset folks will share a similar seminal awareness of the grace of the Park Avenue arbor.

For me, it occurred when I was given a ride in a shiny new convertible one springtime long ago.

Sitting deep in the back of a fat-bodied rag-top at an age when my nose reached the window's edge, I looked up and watched the leaves weave lacy, green patterns through the blue sky along the main artery of town. The canopy went on and on, showing off its glory the entire length of that cresting and falling avenue.

It is one of those timeless images of Manhasset that still captures my fancy in a new century. Those trees have never stopped embracing me, nor have so many others.

I've written about specific Manhasset trees before, the one in a field in the old Chapel Woods with the rope swing, for instance, but I never mentioned the Japanese maple which stood at the side of our Mill Spring Road home. It was an old tree, saved at a time when builders valued preserving such things. It was sturdy-trunked, broad-branched, and to my pint-sized self really, really tall.

It was the first tree I ever climbed. There was a forked branch that allowed me to see clear into a second story bedroom of our house. I read comic books and the Bobbsey Twins' series perched right where my mother could see me from any front window.

Our home on Mason Drive was just by the part of the hill where a view of Manhasset trees underscores the Manhattan skyline. The houses along Mason reside in an arbor of the old Mason Estate - part of which still stood behind our house at 170 until the early 60s.

The estate's fruit arbor is marked by a nearly 300-year-old, white, oak tree that still dominates the crest of Mason Drive. I'll bet some of the berry patches, which grew in a line just beyond that tree through to Nassau Avenue, still bear fruit, too.

I remember the number of huge elms and stately dog-woods that sprawled along the village landscapes before storms, diseases and borers came, wiping out so many and still threatening those that remain.

The cherry trees that swallowed up Manhasset High School each year have been thinned by similar fates; but take the drive toward the school in late April, and the profusion of cherry blossoms from the survivors will stir more than a few memories.

The sycamores suffer, too, a local historian told me. They have to be replaced from time to time due to relatively weak limbs which make them susceptible to weather damage. However, sycamores grow quickly and are often planted as street trees because of their ability to tolerate air pollution and resist disease.

The Manhasset sycamores are cared for and dearly loved, demonstrating appreciation in knobby faces that smile back as if they remember us skating past them on Copley Pond or swinging from the liana vines that wrapped around a forest of hardwood trees at Polliwog Pond in the 1930s.

I am told by those who have lived in Manhasset since its early days that kids rode horses through the woods Frank Munsey bequeathed to the Metropolitan Museum of Art. They'd trot along paths dotted with landmark trees, while houses appeared on streets named for artists: Ryder, Whistler, Rembrandt, Bellows, Hunt.

All of which seems appropriate to a child of this town who got to know the artistry of the environment in its prime, and still finds the outstretched arms of the sycamores welcoming her whenever she returns.

Ode to the Public Library

Early on I felt the silent power books command and it mesmerized me.

The world wasn't so obvious to a child of the 1950s; its secrets weren't spilling from newspapers, radio, television - or adults, for that matter.

When I read a book, I was met with answers to questions I hadn't even formed.

I remember sitting on a tiny stool behind the librarians' check-out area at the Manhasset Public Library in a small cubby-hole section carved out for tots

I'd listen to stories read by volunteers in whispered tones or sit alone, quietly, reading picture books while my mother looked for another John O'Hara or Francis Parkinson Keyes' on the grown-up shelves.

The book I first loved reading all by myself had to do with a little girl named Kiki and her grandfather's garden of sunflowers. That's all I remember.

I can see the book on the "kiddie's library shelf," can remember it to be one of a series, and can imagine it, open in my little girl lap.

I've looked for Kiki in her original spot, as well as online, but can only locate her in my memory now - a warm and welcome guest among the hundreds of other characters from the powerful role books have played in my life.

I don't recall the Manhasset librarian's name, but I've never forgotten her kindness.

In 1957, my father suffered a severe heart attack, his first of two. I was nine.

Dr. Medd arrived at the house in minutes, followed by an ambulance that took my father to the Manhasset Medical Center. Since children weren't allowed to visit ICU patients, I didn't see my dad again for six weeks.

My mother managed a trip to the library during the chaos of that time, and my librarian found me wandering around the non-fiction stacks. In answer to her query about help, I told her I needed to know about heart attacks.

She reached up and pulled a black-covered volume from the shelves.

I read the slim and simple book from cover to cover. Its title was *Thank God for my Heart Attack*. I read it aloud to my father after he began to convalesce at home.

When I was 10, I read Betty Smith's *A Tree Grows in Brooklyn* and never got over it.

At first, I took Francie Nolan's oath and attempted to read all the authors on the fiction shelves, but soon my librarian - just like Francie's - was making selections for me and leading me through Mark Twain and Edgar Allan Poe, and even to Michael Crichton's *The Citadel*.

No challenge was too great because my librarian - again, like Francie's - knew I was a reader of most everything: classics, comic books, MAD magazine, Boys Life, cereal boxes, and bubble gum cards. In fact I had a BFF who always made me promise not to bring any reading material when I spent the night.

In the early 60s, the Manhasset library adopted a new policy and stayed open until 9 p.m. on Monday nights.

Talk about a gift from the gods for Baby Boomer teens! We were rarely allowed out on a school night without written permission from some ruling authority.

Now, we HAD to go to the library. HAD to. There was simply no choice because, suddenly, every teen in Manhasset had reports to research.

We must have driven the librarians insane, and after all this time, let me apologize. During the school year, freedom after the dinner hour was a heady thing for the kids I knew, and we certainly weren't on our best behavior.

For one thing, we showed up in droves.

There weren't enough benches or carrels to contain us, so we stood around the reference section and pretended we were looking up interesting facts in the medical encyclopedias, (a few of which were quite interesting, indeed).

When a librarian had shushed a group too often, she'd shoo them outside and they'd congregate in the parking lot.

It soon became the night version of the 3 p.m. scene outside Town Hall Pharmacy on weekdays.

In order to stay inside, students had to produce mimeographed assignment sheets. We had no trouble fulfilling the requirement, though I don't recall ever completing any of those tasks.

Mostly, we just flirted with the other kids and accomplished some surface research about the mating habits of North Shore, LI Baby Boomers.

I was already comfortable in the library, so Monday nights were a pleasant, social experience for me.

As a result, I developed an even stronger bond with the place, spending countless quiet hours in the school libraries of my life, as well as the public ones.

When teaching high school Seniors, I heard a student brag that he'd never crossed the threshold of a library in his entire life. I had a visceral reaction and, on the spot, offered extra credit to anyone in the class who could produce a library card. It was a dismal showing which led me to extend my offer to all those who could produce one within the next two weeks. I received a thank you note from our local librarian at the end of the offer.

Libraries are man's greatest gift to himself, the treasury of our ideas as long as we've been recording them. Ancient wars were fought over the possession of this kind of knowledge - it was wealth and power combined.

The etymology of the word library is in the Latin word "liber" which is a noun meaning a type of tree bark, thin shavings of which provided the material to make man's ideas portable.

This became a big business in 3 BC Alexandria which fed the papyrus trade with a pledge to collect all the knowledge in the world on scrolls in a building. They actually housed some of the country's greatest scholars who contributed their work - subject to a strict editorial board - in exchange for lodging.

Of course, Alexandria's library didn't offer free circulation to the community at large. Consequently it became an attractive nuisance to pillaging potentates who were jealous of other's possessing such wealth. Not surprisingly, humans have been burning books ever since.

Somehow, through centuries of wars over ideas, libraries have survived.

I don't want to imagine a world where I can't reach for a book that attracts me by its cover, and without spending a dime, borrow it on the good faith that I'll bring it back in one piece.

It's this kind of trust that makes me love the library, still confident that somewhere on those shelves, I'll find another answer - or at least meet friends for life like Kiki, Francie, and my librarian.

SVCC: The Chateau, The Survey, and The Way We Were

Our house on Mill Spring Road was the first one that wasn't part of the Strathmore Vanderbilt community, meaning we weren't entitled to be members of Strathmore Vanderbilt Country Club like the vast majority of our friends' families.

That didn't stop me. For years, I swam in the pool and played tennis with SVCC pals, and since the lifeguard was usually a friend of my brother's, I had access.

SVCC and its vast lawns were a playground to all the area kids, except for the few warm months when we turned it over to the members for their use.

The property was a major point of entry to the "wild side" of Manhasset where all the woods and wonders were. The clubhouse land backed up on Our Lady of Grace, an estate donated by the J. Peter Grace family to the Sisters of the Immaculate Heart of Mary. Before becoming a Montessori school in 1968, it was a favorite prowling spot that led us to roam around the other large estates beyond the Grace fields.

I have been to the Strathmore clubhouse many times - appropriately invited as a guest through the years to holiday shows, birthday parties, summer semi-formals, splash parties, graduation celebrations, showers, weddings, St. Mary's reunions, friend and family memorials.

Consequently in the spring of 2012, when I had lunch as the guest of the SVCC's current manager, Don Feimer, I felt at home.

After an absence of several years, I was struck by the beauty of the drive through the Vanderbilt gates. The azaleas were blooming profusely along the lane and dogwood flowers had just begun to bud. The clubhouse came into soft focus - the slate roof glistening over the soft gray turret and the stone-trimmed windows.

There's a rich history to the more than one-century old chateau and the land on which it stands.

The vast property - as described in today's terms - had borders from the north side of Northern Boulevard, to Searingtown, Powerhouse, and Lakeville roads. The deed was held by the Spreckle family, who still trade in the sugar business and who, at the time, were listed among the wealthiest families of the 19th century in the United States (Spreckles).

According to the SVCC history, the land's title "was conveyed" to a William Chester in 1906 who subdivided the property and developed "country estates" which were purchased by the elite of Manhattan society: the Whitneys, Paysons, Kellys, and Paleys, among them (Strathmore).

A French chateau stood on the remaining land, which appealed to Louis Sherry who'd made his fortune producing confections. The ice cream and candy mogul bought the property in 1914 and vowed to replicate "Petit Trianon," a cottage of Marie Antoinette's in Versailles.

Sherry adorned the rooms with the frills and formalities of the French, and then added grandeur to the grounds with aromatic boxwood gardens, leading to a 40-foot waterfall at the rear of the estate.

After Sherry's death in 1923 the property was purchased by Frank Munsey, a renowned newspaper publisher and the owner of the highly-regarded Munsey Trust Company.

Several historical accounts reveal that Mr. Munsey, an arts' connoisseur, found Sherry's chateau lacking in authenticity.

Munsey promptly demolished the waterfall, added pink brick wings, and an octagonal tower to the house.The cost, for what the the owner deemed true Louis XV style, (which included a hand-painted mural on a ceiling and other amenities), was two-and-one-half million dollars. The project took two years.

Just after its 1925 completion, Munsey died.

Frank Munsey, who had no direct heirs, bequeathed his entire estate to the Metropolitan Museum of Art. The institute kept the property on the north side of Northern Boulevard for a housing development named Munsey Park in their patron's honor. The chateau and 100 acres were sold to Graham Fair Vanderbilt:

"For a decade the property provided a gracious setting for lawn parties and social festivities to which New York's top '400' eagerly responded.

The property was ultimately inherited by Consuelo Vanderbilt, whose interests were focused abroad. In 1939, she sold the house and the 100 acres to the architect/builder, William Levitt, who was gaining prominence in developing various 'Strathmore' communities in Manhasset. Levitt named the new acquisition Strathmore Vanderbilt (Strathmore)."

Levitt turned the chateau and grounds over to the property owners in 1941. A Strathmore Vanderbilt Association was formed to contribute to its maintenance, a fact recorded in bound copies of the community newsletter, *The Survey*, which first appeared a few years later.

Monthly issues recorded the antics and milestones of the community for more than 40 years, ending in the late 1980s when bound copies were turned over to the club's management for safe-keeping.

I spent hours pouring over the Surveys when I visited last spring.

Through the 50s, the newsletters were typed on someone's Royal and, in later decades, on an IBM Selectric, easily identified by its sprawling script font.

The tone of the copy is appropriately chipper or somber, depending on the news of the neighborhood. The color of the paper fits the season and the graphics are line sketches providing transition or humor.

I focused on the issues spanning 1955 to 1965 since those were the years most pertinent to a Baby Boomer's view.

I paged through, looking at the advertisements first because they paint a vivid picture of the town we knew.

Milton Ludecker's Texaco Station reminded readers that they could "trust the man who wears the star."

Anderson's Florist touted that it had "been growing since 1894."

Travelscope suggested a trip to Paradise.

Norman's Bookshop highlighted *Key Witness*, the newest crime thriller from Chapel Road author, Frank Kane, while The Little Brown Shop encouraged the use of its moderately priced, lending library.

Early on, the Surveys were short. The editors reminded homeowners to put up storm windows or to avoid hanging laundry outside on weekends, so as not "to disrupt our little bit of heaven." Gentle rebukes were directed at parents to teach "our dear children not to run through others' gardens and backyards."

The residents wrote notes offering cryptic advice to their neighbors: "Exercise discretion when placing trash at the curb" or issuing polite requests about "containing one's dogs."

The Board of Directors requested that those who drove to the clubhouse: "Leave the keys in the ignition so neighbors, who are inadvertently blocked, can move your vehicle."

Several times each year an editorial begged for more community involvement, asking members to hold family events at the clubhouse to boost patronage or beseeching them to volunteer in restoring the building "to a physical condition of which we can all be proud."

The tactic seemed to work.

By 1958, the Survey's editors were bestowing "Vander-Praises" to a regular group of "VanderGreats", led by Dr. Frank Granito, who not only toiled over the tennis courts and the grounds, but also donated his skills to the plumbing, plastering, and wiring needs of the chateau. Members contributed pieces of fine furniture from their homes to brighten up the foyer and provide more comfortable seating areas.

Even the Gatehouse on the property was cleaned to function as a spot for hosting neighborhood events.

Thirty-seven boys registered to take a boxing class there. Many teens participated in shows directed by Peter Sansone, a student at the American Academy of Dramatic Arts. Peter joined Kay Sillaway and Ruth Desmond, both of whom brought their musical talents from years with Bob Crosby's bands. There were Christmas plays, musical reviews, talent shows, and beauty contests (starring male neighbors in drag).

The Gatehouse became a center for community planning and activity. The "Aquabelles" met there to choreograph the end of summer water ballets. Santa Claus handed out gifts to every child at annual Christmas parties, and well after Easter, one was likely to find an undiscovered, hard-boiled egg hidden in some nook or cranny.

1959 began with normal reminders for the "VanderGuys" and "VanderDolls" to check their calendars for ballroom dancing and bridge lessons, putting contests and fashion shows.

"VanderLaurels" were awarded once again to the tireless Doctor Granito "who, even with his bursitis, readied the tennis courts."

"VanderThanks" were given to those who made a pool table available at the Gatehouse "for the neighborhood boys." However, there was a hint in the copy that things weren't entirely peaceful in SV's "little bit of heaven." The editor added a loaded question about the pool hall: "Will it be appreciated or abused?"

That July a new patio surrounded by rose bushes was installed out by the pool. There were swim races on the Fourth, in addition to a father-son baseball game, a sack race, and a bicycle decorating contest. This was followed by a formal dance which saw Peggy Ernst and Charlie Gallo dance "a flawless Black Bottom," and Regina Beatty jump into the pool for a midnight swim.

The Association reported a summer of record profit at the end of August, along with the somber news that the boys' pool room had to be closed due to "completely unacceptable conduct and actions, including drinking, and broken windows." The Survey's editor wrote: "Perhaps vandalism is a modern expression of youthful exuberance. More likely it's caused by ill breeding, poor training, and weakness. Miscreants become arsonists and endanger lives, making the policing of our property and homes a must. These are not foolish pranks."

Change had clearly arrived, and a few other tidbits in the 1959 Surveys confirmed it.

The first advised that, due to demand, a parking lot was scheduled to open at the LIRR station on Plandome Road: "Stickers are required for the cars of all residents who may then park free of charge."

The second news' item warned that: "a new shopping center to be known as 'Americana' is not a development in keeping with the rest of Miracle Mile and the surrounding community. Efforts to have input about signs, flags, lights, and hours of operation have been met with little success."

Also in the news: Bobby Riggs played tennis on the clay courts to the cheers of a crowd in July, and 23 babies were born to Strathmore Vanderbilt homeowners that year.

The complaints about property destruction continued, however, with neighbors writing in 1962 about the "exploding cut-outs and screeching brakes of marauders" who were called "Nocturnal Hot Rodders," and "perpetrators of deliberate destruction."

The editor opined: "The shocking truth? It's our own kids," further warning, "influences beyond their homes affect them adversely."

But the teens weren't the worst of it. That winter, the unthinkable happened.

It had been a snowy week before Christmas that kept families close to home. After the annual Holiday Show in the Gatehouse, the older kids - dressed as Santa's helpers - played organized games with the little ones while the grown-ups "trekked happily through the snow" to the clubhouse for a Board meeting.

Afterwards the families walked home together, passing holiday doors that had won the decorating contest and Nativity scenes backlit in blue on white-covered yards.

They made particular note of the peace, harmony and safety they felt in their paradise.

Celebrating the season at a large party in the neighborhood later that week, many discovered their empty homes had been robbed of furs, jewelry, and silver by clever thieves who left the police baffled and the cases unsolved.

A shift in perspective took place and police patrol cars were now a regular scene on Strathmore Vanderbilit streets.

Moving forward, the so-called VanderGroups, VanderJuniors, VanderBits, VanderValentines, VanderDancers, and

VanderTeens continued to attend "Charm School" classes for the Regina Cotillion; Square Dances with Chuckwagon buffets; Mens' Nights "with the kind of entertainment men like;" Broadway at group rates totaling $46.50 for six shows; hat fashion parades, and ladies' bowling leagues. The adults danced under the moonlight to Lester Lanin's orchestra; the teens did the stroll with Bobby and the Orbits.

SVCC family life beat through most of the 60s with a new social committee working to add energy to the "all for one and one for all" community bond.

The Survey introduced a new bartender who was a former NYC police officer, noting that he had once served Casey Stengel and Peter Lawford and made "one fine drink."

The Association reminded all that the complimentary canapes offered in the bar were an effort to discourage guests from gathering at homes for cocktails before having dinner at the club.

The editor thanked Newmark & Lewis for the loan of a color television which enabled members to enjoy drinks and a buffet while watching the World Series of Golf.

Through the 70's the rhythm kept its beat with community news, but there wasn't much information about the teens getting together to plan "Splash Parties" and "Harvest Dances."

Operating the facilities and their events got to be too much for the Association at that point, so the club was turned over to a management company which expanded to include non-residents.

Today, Don Feimer says they still deal with kids sneaking around the property in the off-season, but the Gatehouse has been a storage space for years.

The chateau has been freshly refurbished and redecorated, however, with due respect given to its genre and style. It is as cheerful and welcoming as ever.

Kids continue to compete in swim meets and tennis tournaments. The social groups still get together, and the water ballet is, as always, the highlight of every summer's end. High school and family reunions occur in the ballroom on a regular basis.

The management and the membership strive toward encouraging a return to the time when whole families came for entire days during the summer - eating at least one, if not two, meals there with each visit. Those were our days, when the kids all grew up around the pool and then danced at each other's weddings in the club house.

Change has come again, nonetheless.

Brides favor exotic, location receptions these days, and more people own summer homes; more kids go to camp or stay inside to play video games. People like to order food that's delivered so they don't have to dress to go out, and besides, we just don't know our neighbors like we used to - no matter where we live.

In the Surveys there is a running joke about having lived in a house for ten years that is still referred to as the first owner's home. "I know as much about the people who owned this house before we did as I do about anyone currently living in Strathmore," a Survey reader notes.

Another writes: "I love that our house is called by the name of its first owners. It makes us feel like part of the continuum."

That's the way I felt when I sat in the Marie Antoinette dining room last spring - like part of the continuum.

There's life in that feeling; there's longevity in it...maybe even a little bit of heaven.

Spreckles Sugar Company. "History". www.sprecklessugar.com
Strathmore Vanderbilt Country Club. "History". www.strathmorevanderbiltcc.com

The Circle, Games, and Baby Boomer Kids

I'd leave my house on Mill Spring Road bright and early Saturday mornings to get to "The Circle."

As the crow flies, it was close enough for me to hear my father's piercing whistle if I was wanted home, but far enough away to feel like I was being given freedom, with rules of course.

"Stay in the Circle," my mom would always say, "and remember to come home for lunch."

During my first forays to the Circle, I went with Mary, my older sister, who taught me how to get there so that when I went alone, I knew the way.

I cut through the Brennan's, across the street, being ever so careful not to step on the putting-green lawn or in the award-winning garden, keeping to the worn path that brought me to Woodland Way. There the Hurleys always waved to me if they were working outside, before I cut on through their yard to Dr. Green's and half-slid down a steep hill into the Kane's backyard, calling for the Desmond girls, then crossing back over the Vaught's lawn to get to the cul-de-sac officially called Forest Turn.

29

I spent a good nine years playing with the kids whose houses I'd just cut through, and the kids who lived in the houses along Chapel Road, Mountain Cut, or within the Circle itself.

There was a passel of kids, let me tell you.

One house in Forest Turn, where a beloved heart doctor lived with his family, offered ten kids. Putting that group together with the rest of the crowd, we never had trouble fielding teams or devising elaborate games.

An enormous pine tree stood in the middle of the little island that gave the plot its name. The tree was so tall that the youngest among us could stand upright beneath its lowest branches. A hedge surrounded the island's perimeter, creating a cocoon for games like School or House. It was also a perfect place to put a jail when we played Cops and Robbers or a stellar home-base for Hide and Seek or Snow Tag.

I played with the same kids season after season.

They came to our basement to see our first television set. I went to their garages to sit in their dads' new sedans. We laughed until milk came out of our noses in our Levitt kitchens, and argued with our siblings over the one bathroom in the upstairs, center hall which we all had to share.

We staged shows on each other's front lawns for which our parents paid $1 per ticket and played Blind Man's Bluff at each other's slumber parties. We declared ourselves King of the Mountain! on the Big Rocks that were little islands in themselves along Chapel Road, and ran through endless games of Cowboys and Indians in the pine- cozies and wildflower fields of Chapel Woods.

When the right kind of snowfall came, our suicide hill was Mountain Cut, a treacherously steep road that runs into Chapel.

We'd gather at the top with our waxed, Flexible Flyers and shiny aluminum, snow coasters. The big kids let the little kids go down the slower side first - before they took off on an icy path they'd made by pouring water on the other side.

We warded off frostbite in the garages of our neighbors at the bottom of the hill, jumping up and down with tales of the last run we'd made. If we hit the curb or smashed into something, we knew where a mom who was a nurse lived, and if we really had to pee, which mom would let us into her back bathroom.

That's the way neighborhoods operated then.

I know because I played in more than one on a regular basis, and it was rare to be on a street where everyone didn't know your name.

When I was old enough to cross Northern Boulevard on my own, I joined a number of rotating neighborhood kids on Ryder Road between Manhasset Woods and Abbey roads. A BFF lived on Ryder with her three sisters and their dog, Shammy - short for Shamrock - who followed us everywhere, (including into the Manhasset Cinema where he appeared on stage during a movie).

Munsey Park was full of young families who multiplied on a regular basis, so our games of S.P.U.D. and Kick the Can were full of spirit and noise. We'd designate our field, easily marked on the white concrete and black tarred roads of Munsey Park, and "Shoot" to determine the rotation of play. The odd finger was IT.

One summer day in the late 50s, my BFF and her Abbey Road neighbors decided to put on a fair in the woods behind their homes. I helped.

We spent one weekend planning the rides and making signs to post, for what we called, "The St. Francis Hospital Fair" to be held the following Saturday.

We modeled our kid-sized event after the grand "North Shore Hospital Fair," so we designated the new, little hospital on Port Washington Boulevard as our beneficiary.

All activities were ten cents. We pushed kids on swings; pulled them in wagons on the sloping paths through the woods to Bellows Lane and back; sold lemonade and cookies; had a hoop shoot, and other ball toss games. A mom volunteered to paint hearts and stars on cheeks all day.

We raised more than $30 - I'm sure with the help of some extravagant adult tips - and got all dressed up to present the money to the Sisters at the hospital. They served us tea and wrote us a beautiful note about being God's angels on earth.

When my family moved to Flower Hill in 1960, I discovered the Mason Estate - across Old Pine Drive and at the top of Colony Lane.

There was an unimposing, clapboard farmhouse on the property and a few outer buildings including a barn and a small place where a caretaker lived on the lot line that backed up to Nassau Avenue. Orchards stood in neat rows amid the hardwoods.

An old woman lived in the house and we liked to look in her windows, for some reason, as if 11-year-olds need a reason.

That's where the caretaker came in. We'd approach the house from below the orchard so we could duck and hide behind trees while on our mission.

Sometimes we'd get all the way up to the window before the caretaker appeared, clapping boards together, shouting at us to "Get outta here. Now!"

That's what we'd come for, I guess - the incredible rush of getting caught - because I have no memory of the lady inside - only of the cracking sound made by the boards and the caretaker's shouts as we took off.

These imprints are stamped indelibly into my emotional memory. It is the same with fellow Baby Boomers who played at the rock walls, in the circles, and on the big rocks all around Manhasset.

We can go back and look for the world we knew, as I did recently. But in reality, the Forest Turn pine tree is a scrubby, old fir these days, many of the big rock islands have been blasted away to ease traffic issues, and the woods off Bellows and Chapel have long been cleared for the homes that stand there today.

I'm okay with that because in my mind's eye a film plays of how it used to be, and I see all of you there, too.

We're riding our bikes together up and down the hills of our hometown at the first sign of spring, flying over back roads with playing cards clipped to our spokes, hearing the clacks mix with the whistle of the wind. The sycamore buds are bright yellow and the sky is ours to roam. We stop at Sam Asher's to buy an over-priced candy bar for six cents or to yell "Tilt!" at our friends trying to beat Asher's pinball machine.

Or it's winter and we're trudging in rubber boots through the snow with skates hung over our shoulders, heading for Copley Pond. There, we'll struggle on our blades over the bumpy ice at its rim only to glide free on the mirror-smooth ice at the center.

When the warm weather comes, we're marching along Plandome Road in the Memorial Day Parade, or riding our bikes alongside the marchers, aiming at ankles with pea-shooters bought at Gibson's. We're soon on our way to spend an afternoon on the Bay or at the aqua-blue pools of Plandome, Strathmore or North Hempstead - only to end the day waiting for Tommy, the Good Humor man to finally arrive on our streets.

None of us have broken hearts, lost souls, or scraped knees in my biopic, and we're all perfectly whole and happy - maybe it was just in those moments or just in my memory, but it's a romantic comedy I'm watching, so everything turns out just fine.

Love Songs, Miracles, and Loss

My days in the third grade at St. Mary's grammar school were memorable for a number of reasons.

First of all, I was filled with fear about meeting my new teacher.

I'd gone through a school year of petty conflicts with Sister Rosalie in kindergarten, suffered many a trial in first grade with the stern Sister Maria Rita, and I failed to win a royal, May Day nod from our beloved Sister Louisa in second grade. Consequently, I had no idea how third grade would pan out.

Boy, was I surprised.

Third grade held the wonder of all wonders: A young "lay" teacher, meaning one not of a religious order. Her name was Miss Henderson, and she was engaged to be married imminently. So, for the first few months, our lessons were built on the stories of her future plans. We even met her fiancé who came to class one day and surprised her with flowers.

That's not all. We had a classmate who considered himself to be Eddie Fisher's clone and Miss Henderson loved Eddie Fisher, so she allowed us to be entertained by a nine-year-old crooning "O My Pa-Pa," "Lady of Spain," and "Count Your Blessings."

It was all very romantic and third grade girls were literally swooning the fall of 1956. But love in the air wasn't the only cause of weak knees and fluttering hearts.

It was the year the U.S. government ordered Jonas Salk's polio vaccine to be administered to school children from coast to coast. A series of three shots was to be given in the schools by town doctors.

At St. Mary's, an area was arranged in the larger, basement lunch room and classes were lined up against the walls of the first floor hallway. Two queues fed down the stairs and led to one of two doctors, each of whom awaited his next patient with a clean hypodermic at the ready.

Nurses holding antiseptic-laced cotton swabs, and nuns holding the large crucifixes from their rosaries, were poised on either side of the doctors.

The first time we got the shots, even the most brave among us began to hear his knees knock when a few hysterical kids appeared in the hallway held up by nuns or nurses.

One boy bolted for the quickest exit upon seeing an admired friend besieged with terror at the sight of the needle. Another third grader, who'd just received the shot and walked past us with trembling lips, promptly fainted on the staircase, bumping her head on the corner of a step.

The time it took to clear those issues up was just enough to make everyone even more queasy.

Dear Miss Henderson felt our fears and soothed us in a calm voice. She walked along the line saying she would stand behind each of us when we got the shot. I can still feel her hands on my shoulders, planting me in courage.

The second round of shots came a month later - kids were shaking at the mere mention of the date, and though we survived round two with relative ease, we still had the dreadful sounding "booster" to endure.

The adjective meant only one thing to grammar school kids: an even longer and more invasive needle. One that went into your bones, a boy on the playground told us.

Again, it was our brave, third grade teacher - full of love, life, and Eddie Fisher - who had our backs through the deepest puncture.

It was hard to tell whether the boys or the girls loved Miss Henderson more that fall. She was everything we needed - and then some - because we soon realized she was a rabid Brooklyn Dodgers' fan.

Now, just about every Irish, Italian, Polish, German and whatever else American at St. Mary's had a connection to Brooklyn. This included the Immaculate Heart of Mary sisters who were 98 percent behind "D'em Bums."

The holdouts were from the Bronx and rooted for the Yankees. This just made the second, consecutive, subway series a must-see in the new age of television.

The nuns' allegiances translated into a communal bribe: If our classes performed amazing educational feats in record time, we could tune in the games promptly at 2:15 p.m. each day.

Television in school was unheard of in 1956, so the entire grammar school pulsed with ecstasy when we agreed to the contract. Of course, this was all dependent upon classes joining together to find portable television sets to be lent and shared.

No problem for Miss Henderson's class which held the son of a Newmark & Lewis salesman, and the same for his sisters in the fifth and seventh grades. That left other classes - and their dads - to scramble for sets to watch.

It was a great few days of the nuns trading barbs with Yankee fans and then, coming to a reverential silence when their Dodger, Jackie Robinson, was on base. The sisters would grasp their beads and hold them close in mumbled prayer, only to choke the beads tighter when their enemy, Mickey Mantle, was at bat.

We never heard those prayers.

The Dodgers won the first game and the second; one exciting game followed another. The entire school was enraptured, to the point that the bus drivers came into the building to complain about kids not boarding the buses on time, only to find the office empty and the administrators in Miss Henderson's room, cheering a Dodger play with a class full of bus riders.

Don Larsen went on to pitch a perfect game for the Yankees, and the Dodgers lost.

A gloom hung over the playground at recess while we listened to eager Yankee fans crow about their victory.

Our third grade hearts were broken for weeks.

Then they were shattered when we returned from Christmas vacation to find Miss Henderson was gone. She'd "moved away" after her wedding, the Principal told our class.

In the dead silence which followed, the Sister introduced another lay teacher, one much older and more formidable than

Miss Henderson. This one rarely smiled, thought baseball was foolish, and absolutely forbid tributes to Eddie Fisher.

It is only with the perspective of 56 years that I can see Miss Henderson's shoes couldn't have been filled by anyone.

Nothing could top what we'd experienced that fall.

We were the living evidence of Salk's miracle vaccine. We had fallen in love with love. We'd felt the passion of teamwork and the grief of loss.

There was nothing left to teach us, so we spent the rest of third grade daydreaming of the good old days - and making our new teacher's life miserable.

Fountain Pens, Daydreams, and Doodles

There's something you should know about me.

I won the Penmanship Award in the fourth grade.

This may mean nothing to you, if you weren't trained in circling endless ooooo's and eeeee's in your early school years, but then - yes, back in the day - it was an authentic accomplishment.

Penmanship was very important in Catholic School and like most students of handwriting since the turn of the 19th century, we were taught with the Palmer Method.

According to The International Association of Master Penmen, this is an expedient form of handwriting developed by Austin Norton Palmer.

Let me stray here because the backstory is interesting - well, to those of us who are penmanship award-winners, anyway.

Palmer spent years in school perfecting the ornamental handwriting of the era, including time at a New Hampshire business college under the instruction of a famed penman, George Gaskell.

In 1880 Palmer's first job, at age 20, was keeping books with others at the Iowa Railroad Company where, for the sake of expediency and legibility, he began to perfect his method of quick handwriting instruction.

Palmer noticed that the flourishing script of the times required all capitals to be formed with a free-arm swing, while the small letters demanded a time-consuming finger and wrist motion.

The expert discovered one could accomplish much more with "muscular movement," or whole-arm writing, in which one's arm stays on the desk at the elbow with the fingertips no longer controlling the motion of the stylus.

Now, we're talking fountain pens back then - and fountain pens still in the 1950s when I was first introduced to Palmer's Method.

Before we could put pen to paper, we had to learn how to clean, fill, and care for the fragile tool.

When we shopped before the school year began, our supplies included a Schaefer or Waterman fountain pen, a bottle of blue "Quink," and a tiny, brown vial of "ink eradicator."

Imagine the stains on the porous oak desks of our classroom from all those spilled bottles of ink and bursting fountain pen bladders. Not to mention our indigo fingers, the stink of bleach emanating from our mistakes, and the nibs that split from pressing too hard.

No wonder we were required to write JMJ at the top of our papers.

Practicing penmanship was my favorite time during the day, though that wasn't true for my older sister, Mary, who was left-handed. The Method was a right-handed one that

Palmer - and the good sisters - believed could be adopted by all with the "habit" of left-handedness.

The nuns worked hard at breaking Mary's habit and lost.

My sister, who spent the 57 years she was granted in life being true to herself, adapted Mr. Palmer's technique to her left-handedness. She turned her notebook in the correct direction, grasped her pen as the right-handers did, slanted her ooooo's and eeeee's in Palmer-like perfection, and went on to score gold stars and certificates for her accomplishment.

For right-handed, left-brained me - penmanship came easily.

I could get lost in the rhythmic ooooo's and eeeee's, the looping l's and k's, the rounded a's and m's that appeared as if drawn from my pen when it met the paper.

It was doodling perfection. I could daydream and do my classwork at the same time.

Consequently, I took up practicing - doodling - my signature, my alphabet, my numbers, my capitals - on whatever paper was available.

What does Malcolm Gladwell say? We must practice a technique for 10,000 hours to perfect it. Let's see: 8 hours a day, five days a week through college...yeah, I think I had that covered.

So when I became a 12th grade English teacher at Friends Academy in Locust Valley in 1970, I introduced ten minutes of instruction each day to improve my students' skills in legible penmanship.

This didn't go well.

Somehow, I had missed the memo about Mr. Palmer's Method falling out of favor in the mid-60s. The philosophy of elementary education now held that handwriting instruction was more difficult than it needed to be. Printing in an italic style with unjoined letters was far more practical.

At Friends', one student's father - a prominent Manhattan attorney and vocal, tuition-paying parent - typed (get the point?) a letter to the Headmaster about his son "being used as a guinea pig for some new graduate and her inexperienced presumption that upper-level education involves penmanship."

I kept the letter...and my job, by the way. The Head of School handed it to me with a laugh and said:

"I'm on your side, if you want to know the truth. I can't read a damn thing these kids write. However, let's pick our battles on this one. Forget the handwriting lessons, for now."

Today, handwriting lessons in the American school system are more likely to occur in an art class on calligraphy. In 2006, The Washington Post reported in "Is the Handwriting on the Wall?" that only 15 percent of the students who took that year's SAT wrote their essays in cursive.

I'm not surprised.

At the end of my teaching career, students asked me to **print** my notes on the board because they "didn't understand cursive."

I would turn to them and say: "Surely you've heard that I won the Penmanship Award in the fourth grade? I thought everyone knew that!"

And then I'd proceed to doodle my name, the alphabet, my numbers, my ooooo's and eeeee's on the board with enough dramatic flourish to make Austin Norton Palmer blush.

The kids would laugh and smile, not knowing what I knew for sure: I was doodling my way out the door to spend a new lifetime - writing.

Bob Lubbers: Headlights, Thighs, and Embouchure

Robert Bartow Lubbers is best known for drawing many of the sexy women who populated comic strips in the mid-20th century. It is a talent that earned him the prestigious "Yellow Kid Award," presented at the Italian Expo Cartoon Festival in 1998

"I specialize in headlights and thighs," the nonagenarian tells me as we sit in the Marlboro Road home he shares with his second wife, Siegie.

But this isn't that story, so much as the one about how a young Manhasset boy became the professional cartoonist he dreamed of being while growing up in his home on Ryder Road.

Lubbers' story begins in 1930 at the start of the Great Depression. Bob's father, Edward, a banker at 40 Wall Street, managed to pull together three mortgages to secure a home in the newly incorporated Village of Munsey Park.

"What a town," Bob exclaims today. "I was eight and kids my age were everywhere. There were street games, just like we had in Queens' Village, but there were also acres and acres of surrounding dense woodlands, some with meandering bridle paths and low lying vales."

Northern Boulevard was known as North Hempstead Turnpike then, and the defunct tracks of the New York & North Shore Trolley Company were still visible in the pavement a decade after the trolley from Flushing to Roslyn had been replaced by buses.

Groves of ancient hardwoods graced the land east of Manhasset Wood's Road until they met up with the newly-landscaped, Munsey Park Golf Course, not far from its 14th fairway at Copley Pond.

There were commercial centers appearing along the future boulevard, with the Munsey Center in development and Fifth Avenue stores opening closer to Shelter Rock Road.

Locals shopped on Plandome Road, primarily. They had their choice of grocery stores: Bohack's, A & P, King Kullen's, or Andy and Flo's (A&F Market today).

Jaffee's Department store had moved from Spinney Hill to the 800 block of Plandome, just across from the Manhasset Cinema and not far from Milo and George's Ice Cream Shop and Davidoff's Stationary Store.

Pete's sold penny candy in a tiny shop which was south of the LIRR station and across from the solid brick, Plandome Road School.

The Gay Dome bar stood at the corner of Gaynor Avenue and Plandome, hence its name, just a block away from an Esso Station where a gallon of gas sold for pennies. Drivers parked diagonally on all Manhasset streets, sliding in and out of spaces with ease.

Bob started the third grade in 1930. He spent class hours being bored with the 3R's, and drawing WWI Sopwith Camel, Bi-planes like his dad had flown. He created strips of ferocious, machine gun battles pitting Sopwiths against the three-winged Fokker of Von Richtoven, the Red Baron.

For outdoor fun, Bob and his friends scared each other pretending the Onderdonk House was a haunted mansion or during a winter snow, they'd sled down Park Avenue or clear Copley Pond to ice skate.

On summer days they'd make rafts, floating upon them in Polliwog Pond while playing "Huck Finn" or cutting liana vines, drinking their water, then swinging like Tarzan through the hardwood trees.

They played pick-up games of baseball in open fields bordering the grand Shelter Rock Road estates and followed paths laden with blackberries, eating their fill. They discovered Indian arrowheads and looked for red hermatite bowls, then licked them to make "War Paint."

On rainy Saturdays, they headed to the Cinema's double feature, where they watched two movies, a Bugs Bunny cartoon, a Pete Smith Novelty, a Grantland Rice Sports' Special, plus Fox Movietone World News, a travelogue, and the coming attractions - all for 25 cents.

Bob and his younger brother, Eddie, watched a steady stream of moving vans bring families to new houses within days of their completion. Everyone who lived in the Village remarked how the builders had kept their promise: No two houses looked alike.

This was Munsey Park, a development created when the late newspaper mogul, Frank Munsey, bequeathed his entire estate to the Metropolitan Museum of Art. The museum's board had sold 100 acres of his Manhasset holdings to William Levitt and kept the remainder, developing elegant homes on tree-lined streets named for fine American artists.

Construction continued at a rapid pace.

In celebration, 1000 people gathered to watch the Village's fireworks display on July 4th 1931, and that December, Santa Claus made his first appearance at the Abbey Road Circle, a tradition which continues to this very day (Atiyeh, 2).

Finally, however, the stranglehold of the Great Depression began to grip several Munsey homeowners in 1932. They scrambled to save their homes from foreclosure, until Munsey Park drew support from a few hundred residents to form the "Emergency Committee of Munsey Park." The group "collected funds...for the sole purpose of lending aid, unobtrusively, to Munsey Parkers who were on the edge of mortgage foreclosures (2)."

Every penny was paid back.

These are the people who embraced and inspired generations of Manhasset kids like Bob Lubbers who was just a pre-teen, absorbing the world of heroes around him, when he knew he wanted to be a cartoonist.

Jack Abbott's illustrations in the comic strip, "Riders of the Purple Sage" seized Lubbers' attention.

Each night, Bob waited for his father's return on the 25 minute "Banker's Special" from Penn Station. Mr. Lubbers would walk through the door and hand his elder son The Brooklyn Eagle. As Bob recalls:

"The aroma of printer's ink revved me up to read the latest 'Sage' strip. There were beautiful girls in danger and cowboys, with holstered guns slung low, who always came to their rescue. My fascination with drawing airplanes turned into drawing pretty girls. It was a life sentence."

But Bob was still a kid, and he had other fascinations to pursue. One involved a huge oak that had fallen in the woods behind Thayer Road where Les Dittman, the first person to buy a house in Munsey Park, lived.

Bob and his pal, Bud Walters, were enthralled by the tipped stump of tangled roots and clay that remained after the trunk had been cut and hauled away.

In no time they rounded up their 1934 Tootsie Toy mini-model cars, and began carving roads down from the highest level to send their cars on a zig-zag run through the roots. They envisioned a bob-sled-type path, but were having trouble with the curves.

Bob recalls: "That's when Bud's older brother, Phil, appeared, spending a couple of days with us creating a super fast track that sent our cars on a perfect run every time.

We loved Phil Walters. He was born to run street rods, and we used to take some wild rides with him in his car on the old, two-lane, curvy Shelter Rock Road."

Little did Bob and Bud know that Thayer Road's Phil Walters was to become Ted Tappet, who changed his name to prevent his mom from worrying over his days as the hottest midget race car driver on the East Coast. In the 50s, at Le

Mans, Tappet's car left the track for the stands, killing fans on the spot.

Phil never drove in a race again, but Bob saw him years later, back in Manhasset, when Walters was presented an award for sailing mastery. "At that point," Lubbers says, "he still had racing in his blood, but his victories were measured in knots."

Before all that in the late 1930s, Bob Lubbers was busy being a teenager in Manhasset.

He began his cartooning career as a high school student when his art teacher encouraged him to submit drawings to the school newspaper. Lubbers' highlighted MHS sports' heroes in the "Portrait of an Athlete" style of the great New York World Telegram cartoonist, Willard Mullins.

Attracted by the clever illustrations and quips, the editor of the Manhasset Mail coerced Arthur Wright of Wright's Hardware, to pay the young artist $5 a week to create ads featuring comic interpretations of locals. Lubbers' distinct caricatures, of well-known Manhasset folks praising Wright's, increased subscriptions to the fledgling weekly.

During that time, Bob had found an old violin in his grandfather's closet and was soon learning how to play it in the high school's orchestra.

As Bob tells it: "Someone must have heard the sound of music emanating from 189 Ryder because Joe Simmons, a trombonist and MHS junior, called. He asked me to audition for a group being formed by a local clarinetist (Joe Pavlica). They'd been hired to play at the 1935 MHS Senior Prom and already had a drummer, a piano player and a bass fiddler. Joe signed me on. I felt pretty cool - a 13-year old swinging on a fiddle."

This was when radio was king - and Martin Block's show "Make Believe Ballroom," was listened to by every teenager in the metropolitan area. The song of the day was "Goodie, Goodie":

"So ya met someone who set ya back on your heels. Goodie, goodie.

So ya met someone and now ya know how it feels. Goodie, goodie."

The song had swept the country by storm, but the sheet music wasn't available yet.

"So, we played it by ear," Bob remembers. "You know, like Dixieland - right from the heart, with some frisky fiddle harmonics. 'Hoo-ray and Hallellujah, you had it comin' to ya'. Goodie, goodie for you...' Wow! That MHS prom was a blast."

Soon enough however, Bob ditched the fiddle for a trombone and joined the MHS Marching and Concert Bands. It would turn out to be a wise choice.

"Ever since, that was it," he says. "All the good things in my life came to me through two things: music and art. One would be my long life's career, the other my lifelong hobby."

It was in his MHS art class that Bob met Grace Oestreich, who had been born in town at 30 Summit Drive, but Bob had never seen her before that day in high school.

The two became inseparable. They talked and flirted so much, the teacher sent them to another room where their romance blossomed.

Then came more music as Bob worked on his embouchure.

Hearing a pitch on the "Tommy Dorsey Radio Hour" for brass musicians to play in an amateur hour, Lubbers reported to 30 Rockefeller Center in the city to audition in 1938. He walked down the hall carrying his trombone and a toilet plunger cap, hoping they wouldn't ask him to read music and hardly noticing Boris Karloff was walking towards him.

Lubbers played "Wabash Cannonball" and won $75, which his father matched so Bob could buy a 1934 Ford Phaeton. The car provided transportation to his new gig, playing with a band at the White Horse Tavern on Post Avenue in Westbury.

Bob was feeling good. He had a car. His cartoons were a hit. He had a beautiful girlfriend, a regular music gig, and an open invitation to play with the groups who made the MHS GO dances jive. It just didn't get any better.

Sometimes while playing at those dances, he enjoyed the best of two worlds. He'd blast a hot Lindy "for the MHS jitterbuggers," then sit out a slow tune to dance "cheek to cheek with my girl."

After the GO dances, he and Grace would drive all the way over to Jericho Turnpike's Howard Johnson's to sample a few of those 28 ice cream flavors.

Or else they'd go to Milo and George's and get a hand-packed pint of vanilla, with two wooden spoons, for 50 cents. On those nights Bob and Grace would share the treat while "schmoozing in the Phaeton after riding through a secret entry off Plandome down a two-rut, dirt trail to a little beach where the moonlight glistened on Manhasset Bay."

When he wasn't with Grace, he was answering the call of the LIRR trestle challenge which seemed to have been heard by all Manhasset boys for a number of decades.

The rite of passage in Bob's time involved a teen boy walking across the rickety expanse, 100 feet above the estuaries of the Bay, to Great Neck - while a train was coming towards him.

Lubbers recalls flattening himself against the trestle's fencing, feeling the horrific shake and the long whoosh of the train as it passed. When it was over, with his heart pounding in his chest, he felt an overwhelming sense of accomplishment.

I asked him if this made him eligible for a fraternity. He quipped, with his 91-year-old blue eyes shining: "Not unless it was 'I Felta Thigh.'"

Following high school, Lubbers followed his art teacher's advice again and was accepted into the prestigious Art Students League on 57th Street in Manhattan. Known for its founding by artists in 1875 to be "run by artists for artists," the classes provided Lubbers with the fundamentals he needed to launch his career as a cartoonist. He studied for two years with famed instructors like George Bridgman, but one day the time came to leave:

"My pal Stan Drake [also an accomplished cartoonist] and I left Bridgman's life class, marched down to Centaur Comics, and sold the comic mag features we'd created. Before long I was doing features at Fiction House."

Best known for its pin-up style "good girl art," Fiction House and Bob's years of drawing headlights and thighs were a natural blend, until World War II broke out just after Bob had married his girl, Grace.

Bob says what followed was an incredible string of seren-dipitous events that framed his life.

First, remembering his father's WWI flights, he signed on with the U.S. Air Corps, even though Ken Molloy and the rest of Manhasset's eligible youths were enlisting in the Navy.

Bob trained to be a waistgunner, but got switched from a crew at the last minute to fill in for a radio operator on an-other run.

Lubbers' originally scheduled flight went down in a Ger-man field where the farmers pitchforked the entire crew to death. He knew he'd drawn a lucky straw on that mission and the rest he flew - unlike the seven Manhasset boys who never made it home from the war.

When it was all finally over Fiction House welcomed Lub-bers back, a small stroke of serendipity that was followed a few years later by perfect timing.

In 1950, Lubbers' mentor - Abbie an' Slats cartoonist, Rae-burn Van Buren - told him the Tarzan artist at United Features was leaving.

Thinking back to his younger days of swinging on Munsey Park liana vines, Lubbers made up a sample book that won him the job and an eventual membership in the National Car-toon Society, "where I met all my heroes," Lubbers says.

From there, Bob's life was sheer good fortune.

Soon he and Grace started a family with the birth of their daughter, Wendy, in 1953 which was followed in no time by a huge break.

In 1954, Lubbers met Al Capp, the mega-star creator of *L'il Abner*, who asked him to "Come up and see me at Noon tomorrow. I'm at the Waldorf Astoria."

Lubbers waited in the lobby "forever," until Capp finally rang for him to come to his suite. On his way in the door, Bob was passed by a very disheveled looking blonde on her way out.

"Capp gave me a great shot to draw with his studio of artists," Lubbers recalls, adding that those years put him into a whole new world of driven New York artists.

In time Lubbers became one of them, writing and drawing the story lines of as many as five different strips a day. His work covers an amazing spectrum of images from *The Saint* to *Secret Agent X-9* (as Bob Lewis), and *Long Sam* - a gorgeous hillbilly imagined by Al Capp, but given life by Bob Lubbers.

The daily newspapers had a six week lead and Sunday editions, only two weeks; Lubbers was always on deadline for something.

As hectic as they were, Lubbers has amazing tales of the those days.

On the dark side, there are yarns about receiving Capp's "cigar-stinking packets of vulgar ideas that I'd have to clean up every week," and the insanity of the many years Capp hid in a hospital while under investigation for two sodomy charges by college girls.

But there are also bright stories about the fun times. There was the day Carol Burnett called to say she loved his work or the night he, Grace and Wendy had front row seats at

Broadway's production of *L'il Abner* with Julie Newmar playing Passionata Von Climax.

Back home in Manhasset, Grace gave birth to Robert Winters Lubbers in 1958, and Bob joined North Hempstead Country Club in 1959. There, he played golf twice a week with a foursome that included his dear friend, John Gambling Sr., until the WOR radio host's death.

The years passed. Bob went to the games at MHS fields, stood on Plandome Road cheering the marchers in all the parades, and couldn't believe it when his kids graduated from MHS, as he and Grace had done.

He rode the same train his dad had ridden into the city, and came home to the same town. Manhasset remained static until the 1980s when little changes took away landmarks and big money tore down perfectly fine center-hall, Colonials to build mega-mansions with three-car garages.

But Bob didn't change; he is still all about art and music.

He has been known to scoop up the mud from a brook to sculpt it into Grace's profile on the spot. Once on a whim, he created a crossword puzzle that was not only published in the New York Times' Sunday Magazine, but which also appears in a bound copy of the 50 greatest puzzles of all time.

He played the trombone well into his 70s and, in his 90s, is working on restoring his embouchure.

While I'm visiting with him he shows me a graphic book he illustrated tracing the history of his mother's family.

Isabelle Bartow's tree dates back to 1683. Bob's beautifully drawn story tells of the Barteau's escape from France to a farm in Flushing before settling in Huntington, and later, Brooklyn.

That's all before Isabelle moved to Manhasset in 1930 with her husband and two boys to find a future in the newly incorporated Village of Munsey Park.

More than 80 years later, Bob is still here. He lost "his sweetheart Grace," in 2000, 62 years after they met and 57 years following their marriage.

But there was another bit of serendipity in store for Lubbers in his 80s when he met Siegie Konrad while taking an art class in Manhasset.

Siegie lived in Manhasset, too, but they'd never met before - and just like the first time he met a sweetheart in an art class and married her - Bob hasn't left Siegie's side since.

We sit around the dining room table in their Marlboro Road home and enjoy a delightful lunch filled with stories, most of which you'll have to wait for because this multi-talented artist is currently writing a memoir about his days as a cartoonist.

This is his Manhasset story - the one about a boy who loved to draw and play music - who was raised in a village built by an art museum where giving your neighbor a hand up set the tone for the generations that followed.

Atiyeh, Phillip. "A History of Munsey Park." http://www.munseypark.org/village-history

STALKING BOYS

I love to follow the strains of conversations on a Facebook page entitled: "I grew up in Manhasset."

Oh, the tangled inter-web we weave.

A chat about matchbook covers extends from the irony of our first cigarettes being lit by matches from the local pharmacy, and on from there to an exchange about reunions at the old Publicans on the Pier. That memory strikes up a connection among three friends who go off on another Manhasset tangent.

I know we could never make these contacts in real time - possibly not even if we all still lived in the same old town.

But on the wonderfully named "web'" we weave links that are cosmically drawn.

Like my new Facebook pal who turned out to be the MHS girl friend, and long-time wife, of my, now deceased, Jones Beach love from Whitestone (see first Manhasset Stories book).

Now what are the odds?

Not to mention, this same woman is the sister of a heart-throb of one of my best, forever friends.

Did you get that?

In our youth, the heart throb drove his very own, sleek black Chevy past Town Hall Pharmacy like James Dean himself. He was older and he tooled around town a lot.

I know because we followed him.

Yes. I'm admitting in my 60s that there are men today who, as Manhasset youths, were observed closely by a group of SMHS girls who had perfected the art of spying.

Sort of.

We had limited equipment.

For instance when we followed our Manhasset James Dean, we were usually in an enormous 1959, white-finned Cadillac, our friend's family car.

Remember: Few of us had cars of our own to drive. We drove what was available at the moment.

I doubt we could have been more conspicuous in such a huge Caddy. I'm not sure we even got close enough to talk to this stud in the early years of my friend's infatuation; but, we kept tabs on him.

We also worked on our feet, and many of the boys we stalked lived in our immediate neighborhoods.

One was a close friend of my Whitestone love.

He was a gorgeous, long-lashed boy with thick black hair and a name that set the rhythm to a song of our generation. "Aiy-yi-yi-yi," we'd sing along with the chorus that chanted his name.

A girl friend, who had been voted Most Humorous in the SMHS Class of '65, was ceaseless in her love for, and pursuit of, this boy.

We watched him on his dates, sometimes sitting in the back of the Manhasset Cinema when he was a few rows in front of us. We also spied on him at a party to which we hadn't been invited, but where we hid in the bushes after sneaking through a few back yards.

It sounds kind of pathetic, but it was loads of fun.

One dark night, we had the audacity to creep into Aiy-yi-yi-yi's back yard.

We followed the lit windows of his house and saw him sitting on a couch in his basement watching television, with his arm around a girl of extraordinary beauty.

My forever friend, the one smitten with Aiy-yi-yi-yi, decided we should drop her into the window well so she could sneak a closer peak.

Uh-oh.

Just as we were lowering her by her wrists into the deep well, we heard Aiy-yi-yi-yi say "What was that?" and saw him jump up from the couch.

When we let go, we told our spy to "Hide! We'll come back."

We ran faster than I knew we could, jumping over tree stumps, scurrying past neighbors who were walking their dogs, and collapsing on some grassy hill in adrenaline-fueled giggles.

Aiy-yi-yi-yi didn't follow us very far once he realized we were just a bunch of stupid girls. So it was easy to creep back to rescue our spy while Aiy-yi-yi-yi was, most likely, explaining our idiocy to that beautiful girl.

It was all pretty harmless, and we never left any evidence behind, like toilet paper covered trees, as teens do today.

Oh, wait a second.

I do recall that a few guys left a calling-card at the location of a girls' slumber party in the mid-60s. In the morning, all the girls were laughing at the front bay window. The hostess' father was out on the front lawn, shaking his head and cursing, while he pulled hanging prophylactics from his Strathmore Vanderbilt azaleas.

Wall Phones, Long Cords, and Party Lines

The telephone number of my youth was Manhasset 7-5151. Area codes didn't arrive until the mid-60s because most people only had one line before that, and possibly, a telephone on each floor of their homes.

We had a wall-phone in the finished basement, another on a wall in the kitchen and a third - a black, desk phone - in my parents' bedroom. The kids weren't really allowed to use this one. It sat on a mahogany "telephone table" that had a matching chair. Most of the homes I visited had one of these some place.

All had dial phones, of course, and dial we did.

Since there was no "call waiting," the caller had to dial and redial - then redial, again and again - to get through to a friend with a busy signal.

I was capable of doing this hundreds of times if the message I needed to convey to a friend was important enough, as all seemed to be.

MA 7-2268. MA 7-2268. MA 7-2268. Endlessly my index finger turned that dial.

The girls in that house never got off the phone.

The same was true of my beloved friend, MA 7-4408, who had three sisters. It was virtually impossible to get through to her, and if one of her older sisters answered, she was likely to say my friend wasn't allowed to come to the phone.

The father of these four beauties finally succumbed to installing a telephone with a separate number - just for the girls - on the landing at the head of the stairs.

He often said the plastic handle was going to wear out in record time because the phone was in perpetual use.

Just as a case in point, in most Baby Boomer homes the telephone was a family item, used in a communal space.

"Don't you whisper into that phone!" was a common remark cast toward a kid whose phone cord couldn't be stretched far enough away from an adult.

I resorted to speaking "Double G" with my friends when on the phone in the presence of authority.

"Whitta-gut ditta-gid yitta-goo gitta-get kitta-galled titta-goo thiitta-ghee itta-goff-itta-giss fitta-gor?" I'd say into the receiver in a clear voice.

This drove my mother insane.

So my 1959 Christmas list included Ma Bell's new "Princess Phone" for Santa to have installed in the room my sister and I shared.

"It's little...it's lovely...it lights."

Marketed as a bedroom phone, the sleek design allowed it to be placed easily on a nightstand, and it came in pink.

The Princess didn't appear under our tree, but MA 7-0146 got one and there was truly nothing like it. I started going to her house just to have the Princess Phone experience.

Back at my house, the favored phone was outside the basement laundry room near our brand-new Magnavox TV. The phone had a long cord, so even if people were watching television, I could snake into the adjacent laundry room to have some privacy.

Sometimes, I could even close the door.

I needed to be alone because my friends and I had discovered, at the age of 12, "party lines."

I'm sure there was more to the party than the game we created on these open lines which delivered constant static when we connected to them. Somehow, we avoided any complications because we had our own agenda.

Kids hollered over the noise to each other.

It was like getting in touch with another planet. You'd hear people shouting phone numbers over and over. Then they'd hang up to see who'd call them.

My friends and I quickly realized we could scream anyone's phone number into that static.

So we did.

We shouted the numbers of the St. Mary's convent and the Church rectory, which we already knew by heart from all the prank calls we'd dialed their way (no *69 then).

"Is your refrigerator running, Sister?" Ha- ha.

Can kids perform prank calls these days? I'm not sure.

What a shame. There's nothing like a harmless prank call that works.

Like calling a number and telling the person you're from the telephone company and men are working on some extremely important lines close by, so please don't answer the phone if it rings within the next two minutes."It's not likely," we'd instruct authoritatively, "but picking up the phone could cause an electrocution."

So at 1minute 55 seconds we'd call back. We'd let the phone ring and ring. The homeowner wouldn't pick up. Then at 2:01 we'd call again, the phone would be answered, and we'd let out a blood curdling scream.

Ahhhhh. Good times.

In high school my outgoing calls from home were to girls, mostly. It was a day and age when girls didn't call boys.

Girls waited by the phone for boys to call us. It was grueling. I waited often.

We only called a boy to see if his line was busy which might explain why he wasn't calling us. But a perpetually busy line meant so many things: was a female on the phone in his house, did he take the phone off the hook, or was he on the phone with MA 7-2259?

There was another important rule to this phone etiquette: If the boy's phone rang and someone answered, we'd hang up.

Since I had an older brother, I knew first-hand how this drove parents crazy.

We'd hear our mother speaking into a void: "Hello...Hello? Oh, not this again. Please either stop calling or speak up..."

The phone was as central to our existence then as it is to teens today; but the phones we used were installed in the walls and the numbers we called had limited availability, imposed by humans as well as technology.

For instance, each day I called the same circle of girlfriends the minute I got home from being with them at school.

It was time-consuming to reach one of them

When I got 'a busy' from MA 7-2268 and MA 7-2259, I figured they were talking to each other. I made this deduction because MA 7-7132 was grounded, and I'd called MA 7-4408, only to be told she wasn't allowed to come to the phone because it was "homework time."

See, the main difference with the phones of the Baby Boomer years was, a parent could answer the phone and deliver an ultimatum or pick up an extension and say: "I told you to get off the phone and come to dinner."

I never had a friend whose parents didn't do that.

Even MA 7-0146's Princess phone and the four beauties with the private number found themselves without instruments from time to time. Their fathers, fed up with the constant jabbering, had each been known to unplug the four-pronged jack from the wall, insuring silence for awhile.

Somewhere along the line, I lost my fascination with spending time on the phone. It may have started at 40 when I didn't have my mom to call anymore, but it ended for sure when my sister, Mary, was no longer there to share events with.

There is no landline at our house these days. Only telemarketers called that number, so I just use my cell phone now.

I have to say, I don't find the architecture of my iPhone particularly comfortable for lengthy conversations, and besides, we're still asking: "Can you hear me now?" no matter the server or the instrument.

My kids tell me they use phone calls for business mostly, otherwise they text their friends. I like texting, too, but it certainly has its limits.

I imagine we'll all be Skyping and using Face Time more in the future, which in my case requires make up.

At that point, I'll be longing for the days when we could pull the wall phone's long cord into the laundry room and get a little privacy.

Questions, William Levitt, and Knowing Better

I was that kid who always wanted to know "Why?" "You question everything," my mother used to say to me, and I wanted to know why she used 'question' as a verb.

My queries drove the adults in my life to 'shush' me or pass over my raised hand at the end of a class lesson.

In time I found answers myself in the Collier's Encyclopedia on the shelves of our living room, or in the "Reference" section of the Onderdonk Avenue library.

I discovered quickly that there is an invisible trail of cookie-crumble questions that keeps the curious on a search without end.

Writing the first book of Manhasset stories raised so many questions for me, some mundane and others, most important.

Consequently, I spent a good deal of time reading through histories of Long Island, visiting Long Island museums, and talking with Long Island friends and family to reclaim a stronger sense of the place that holds my roots.

I also logged many an hour at the Manhasset library scrolling through the mid-20th century microfilm of Manhasset weeklies, the Press and the Mail.

I was usually looking for something I knew had happened. I just wanted some facts to back the event up.

Like the Soap Box Derby in which my brother, Jim, participated around 1953 or 54.

Jim remembers that he built his car without any help from our father realizing, just before the race down Mason Drive, that he hadn't installed the steering mechanism correctly. His pre-pubescent brain figured he'd just remember to steer the opposite of the way required. Well, need I say how that turned out?

However, I was curious to see what else happened during that race of homemade boxcars held so long ago.

So I turned to the microfilm, a dizzying experience of rolling through gray, often blurry pages.

The problem? With all those wedding announcements, celebrity appearances and ads-of-old rolling by, I was instantly driven off the Soap Box Derby track.

I couldn't resist the advertisement about The Little Brown Shop throwing a Girl Scout party to celebrate their new Scout Department or the one about three Manhasset High School sororities - ATA, AZP, and APB - hosting fall teas.

I can't help drifting to these topics. I want to know about Leslie Caron's visit to North Shore Hospital in 1953 with Mrs. William Paley, or that Ethel Merman swam in a one-woman, water ballet in Sea Cliff and more than 20 Manhasset ladies attended.

At any rate, I was having trouble pin-pointing information on the Soap Box Derby and couldn't find confirmation of the event anywhere, except in another racer's memory - and all he recalled was the fact the event existed.

Nonetheless I just kept reading the microfilm ads for Yore Cleaners, J.J. Newberry's, Lilliput Nursery School, Calderone's Pharmacy, The Party Shop and Olive Duntley Florist's.

Of course, I stumbled over the hard news, too: fatal car accidents, boys leaving for war, or vocal anti-Communist campaigns.

The 1952 newspapers touted headlines like "Commie Plans for Ruling America." The story recorded an event hosted by the American Legion for a "near capacity house in the MHS auditorium." An editor of Counter Attack magazine spoke, warning the audience of Communists infiltrating American communities as "spies and saboteurs."

I stopped short when I saw a story about air raid sirens being installed outdoors around town. Baby Boomers clearly remember those towering speakers, and the strange bomb drills we had in school after they appeared.

However, I had no recollection of another part of the story, probably because I was only 5 years old at the time.

One evening in 1953, Manhasset residents underwent a "hypothetical baby atomic bomb drop" at 7:45 p.m. when all the town sirens, horns and whistles sounded the alarm, meaning: "expect an attack at any minute."

Historical tidbits that appear on the Facebook page "I Grew Up in Manhasset" also attract my attention. They might involve something I hadn't known before. I become curious and my desire to question kicks in.

Two pieces of information surprised me.

The first was this: William Levitt's early deeds contained race-restrictive covenants.

Research led me to discover clearly discriminatory language in deeds from other Levitt developments, though I couldn't find the exact wording of a Manhasset covenant. However, those deeds are mentioned in the book *Inside Culture*.

Sociologist David Halle records that 200 houses built by Levitt on the old Onderdonk Estate by 1934 were "deeded to exclude Jews." Ironically, Levitt was a religious Jew who lived in Manhasset himself. Nonetheless, Halle notes that race-restrictive clauses were common in deeds issued by American suburban developers until well after World War II (229).

The second fact I never knew was that it took a class-action lawsuit against the Manhasset Board of Education for the students at Manhasset's Valley School, which was primarily populated by African-Americans, to achieve equality.

In the U.S. Court's 1964 decision of Blocker vs. the Board of Education, the Valley School was closed. Celebrating with a victory march, parents walked their children down Spinney Hill to attend the Plandome Road School for the first time (Johnson and Means).

When I was a child I never thought much about how white my world was or, in my late teens, how diverse my world became when I went to college. I'm amazed that these indignities swirled all around me while I went on my myopic, merry way, but I feel better knowing about them now. My career in education taught me that we have to know where we came from and what made it so. A sense of place strengthens one's back bone.

Baby Boomers are children of the Silent Generation. When we wanted answers, we had to find them, and then - thanks to a legion of teachers like Maya Angelou - when we knew better, we did better.

I came from a time when there were so many unanswered questions, into a time when most answers are literally at our fingertips.

I can only hope that will make us smarter, a whole lot sooner.

Halle, David. Inside Culture: Art and Class in the American Home. Chicago: University of Chicago Press, 1993.
Johnson, Dedrick and Means, Lloyd. Spinney Hill: The African American History of Manhasset and Great Neck. New York: CD-Rom, 2011.

Bruce Scotto: House-hunting, History, and Home

Bruce Scotto was 12 years old when he began his training in real estate. It was to become the most enriching career of his life, he just didn't know it for at least 40 more years.

However, Bruce's interest developed when Salvatore Scotto decided to move his wife, the former Eva Castrulli, and three sons to Manhasset from Brooklyn.

On New Year's Eve 1961, Bruce was the only family member willing to go on another hunt for a house in Manhasset. So, young Scotto was his dad's wing man when the owner of 150 Lindberg Street accepted Salvatore's $23,500 bid.

Mrs. Scotto was shocked to have been left out of the process, but Bruce remembers his thrill at having been included.

Today, after a timeline of jobs that has been an adventure in itself, Bruce has nestled into a comfortable place providing Title Services for many of Manhasset's real estate transactions. He has also adopted a second occupation: Bruce is an online docent for Manhasset's cultural history.

We're sitting with our spouses in the town's Tender Bar when Bruce recalls those long, familial house-hunting trips. He remembers making note of Manhasset's ancient houses of worship and revolution; the rolling hills of horses and manses; the huge rocks appearing randomly amid gracious pre-WWII Colonials, and the canopies of trees adorning streets along the way.

His new appreciation for architecture was further enhanced, shortly after the Scottos moved to Lindberg Street, when Bruce visited the home of his first Manhasset friend, Rusty Prutzman. Rusty's father, a Hollywood attorney, had moved his family from Forest Hills to 128 Summit Avenue.

The house had been built in the 1920s, expansively designed for the family of Eddie Cantor, a mega-star of stage and screen. Bruce remembers an area upstairs that was referred to as "the children's living room." It was adjacent to several bedroom suites. Downstairs there was a butler's pantry and an extensive library. Bruce recalls at least 20 rooms, plus a swimming pool in the backyard.

He was fascinated. This kid from Brooklyn was certain a world of possibility had opened up for him, and he set out to explore it

Scotto got to know his Lindberg Street neighborhood first. One of Manhasset's great, pocket neighborhoods, the small community sits below the railroad bridge at the bottom of Mason Drive. Bruce's first job, walking an elderly neighbor's dog for $2.50 a week, gave him an indelible, streetwise perspective of Baby Boomer suburban life.

By 1964, he was riding his bike up and down the streets of Flower Hill delivering the Long Island Press, before changing to a Newsday route in North Strathmore, further imprinting the streets and homes of Manhasset on his brain. It was a map that he would fill in with each move that followed, and there were more than a few.

The Scottos bought a larger house on Shorehaven Lane in 1964, but Salvatore Scotto's father died in 1965, making it clear they'd have to find one even larger to accommodate his aged mother.

Another hunt for Manhasset housing began, this time, for property upon which to build a house. Salvatore Scotto found a rare piece on Shoredale Road and became his own contractor.

While all this was transpiring, Bruce had turned 16. He was going to Manhasset High, eating cheeseburgers at Town Hall Pharmacy, wandering the aisles of Phil's Sports' Shop, spending beach days at West End 2, daring death at the Port Washington sand pits, and taking St. Mary's girls to MHS dances and the Manhasset Cinema.

With working papers in hand, he landed a real job behind the soda fountain at Lamston's five and dime store on Northern Boulevard, a mecca for St. Mary's grammar school kids who, with hands full of coins, stood six deep behind the counter at 3:03 p.m. on weekdays.

Bruce lasted a week before scoring a job, through his Gull's Cove friend Jerry Izzo, in the receiving department at Lord & Taylor's. It was a far less hectic atmosphere.

Meanwhile, "to test the market," Bruce's impulsive father put the newly-built Shoredale Road house up for sale, and had an offer before the paint was dry.

The results further wetted Mr. Scotto's appetite for Manhasset property, but dampened Eva's hopes of solving their housing issues because, at precisely the same time, Salvatore had also sold the crowded Shorehaven Lane house they were living in. He promptly bought a 5 bedroom Colonial at 3 Vanderbilt Avenue. It was a house that became too large almost immediately when the boys started leaving for college.

For Bruce it was Windham College in Vermont, a place that only one thing could drag him away from each summer: The Best Manhasset Job Ever.

From 1969-1973, Bruce drove the night shift for Harold Powell's Taxi Company, located at the Manhasset LIRR Station. His 3:00 p.m. to 2:15 a.m. shift was during the era of "The Bar Car" when the LIRR gave weary commuters permission to party all the way home from the city.

The work arrived with the commuter trains, but in between those, the drivers talked. Harold Powell, a fascinating business man, loved to tell his family's story of coming to Spinney Hill in the early 20th century, about the same time the Jaffee family was opening its first dry goods' store on East Shore Road.

Bruce repeats his memories of Powell's story with reverence, saying his boss was "one of the most interesting and one of the kindest men" he's ever known.

Powell, born in upstate New York around 1907, grew up on Spinney HIll, graduating from Manhasset High School and attending Columbia University's School of Engineering in the 1930s. To help pay his tuition Powell bought a car, intending to operate it part-time as a taxi in Manhasset.

As Bruce recalls, Powell said "the taxi bug bit him," and Harold was soon engineering a whole taxi fleet that served passengers disembarking from LIRR trains on Plandome Road.

In the early days Powell's weekend clientele was made up of an elite group who were invited "to weekend" at the Gold Coast estates in town. Celebrities like Barnard Baruch, Charles Lindbergh, and Fred Astaire were regular partiers at Jock Whitney's "Greentree" estate on Shelter Rock Road.

Whitney's extravaganzas were legendary among the cabbies of Manhasset in the 1930s who kept themselves up to date with the latest news. They traded horse racing tips with the trainers en route to Greentree's stables, while picking up celebrity gossip from the housekeepers needing a lift back to the main house after a day off.

It was the talk of Manhasset that Jock Whitney, a major investor in Gone With the Wind, was escorting Vivian Leigh to its Atlanta premier; and everyone who enjoyed a drink in the local bars knew about the romance going on in Whitney's guest house. A married Manhasset celebrity regularly called for a cab to take her to Greentree, just after her celebrity husband boarded a train to the Manhattan.

Scotto recalls a great celebrity taxi tale of the 60s that came from Ruggiero's driver and Manhasset friend, Tommy Meehan (aka "Chapter 13" The Tender Bar).

A call came in early one Sunday morning to pick up David Niven at JFK and drive him to the Paley Estate, "Kialua Farm." Niven told the driver, a Mr. Dauenhauer of Manhasset, that he was hungover. Hearing this, Mr. Dauenhauer replied that because it was Sunday morning, even the legendary bars of Manhasset weren't serving yet. However, he had a bottle back at his house from which they could share "a nip of the horse that bit him."

As Scotto tells it: "A short while later the two were sitting in the Dauenhauer living room enjoying a little cheer when Mrs. Dauenhauer awoke, walked in wearing her night gown, and nearly keeled over when she saw David Niven."

Bruce also remembers the one about the time a night nurse was sitting in the back of a new van on her way to work at the Manhasset Medical Center, talking endlessly to the driver, and then becoming suddenly silent after the left turn through the green light onto Northern Boulevard.

Craig, the driver, immediately realized the "Suicide Doors" on the van's passenger side had flung open, depositing the nurse - unharmed - into the street by St. Mary's.

The Manhasset taxi stories keep coming.

Bruce drove Bernie Madoff, though not notable in the 70s, to Roslyn regularly. He also took Al Lewis, the beloved Grandpa Munster, to his monthly appointments with a North Shore dentist for awhile.

But Scotto had a Sunday night fare who was a favorite. Her name was Ollie, and she'd arrive at the station on an evening train, fresh from her night off as a maid at the Marshall Estate. Ollie always asked Bruce to drop her at The Office on Plandome Road for a quick one before driving her back to work at 7:30. Sometimes, Bruce sat with her at the bar and let her talk while she enjoyed her beer. He doesn't remember much of what she told him, but he knew it made her feel good to have someone listen.

Other nights, after his last fare in the wee hours, Bruce walked down from the station to The Cave where Buddy Kilmeade pulled him a long draft and they watched night-time Manhasset go by until "Last Call." Bruce remembers Kilmeade's as a place run with loving care by folks who "knew how to take care of their own. They were the salt of the earth."

I can attest to Kilmeade's fame. I was once sitting in an Atlanta bar in the 90s when a group started naming "the best bars ever." Out of the blue, one of the guys said: "I was in this Long Island place called The Cave where everyone knew each other. They all kept buying me beers." Of course, it was Kilmeade's, yet another Manhasset "Tender Bar."

To further Bruce's evolution as a historian and raconteur, he worked a second job the summers of '72 and '73 at Port Washington's Ghost Motorcycles, owned and lorded over by the legendary Sal DeFeo.

Few could miss the attraction of Sal's lot full of bikers on Port Boulevard; however if, for some reason, one's eyes weren't drawn to that sight, it was because Sal had just driven by on his Harley with the attached side-car adorned by a beautiful girl or his dog, Chico.

Bruce remembers that the cast of regulars at Ghost was "truly classic." In particular he recalls two Italian mechanics.

One held a profound belief in the veracity of wrestling and the absolute trustworthiness of his hero, Bruno Sammartino. After Scotto remarked casually that wrestling was fake, a crescent wrench whizzed just past his head.

And then there was the day a Brooklyn mechanic, who talked like a 1930s' Sicilian gangster, turned out to be the 70s version in reality.

The Immigration and Naturalization Service showed up at Ghost with a warrant to search the mechanic's shady-looking, Mercedes 300SL. They found two hand guns, a machine gun, and a very phony car registration, prompting the Italian's arrest.

Bruce says that upon being asked why the weapons were in the trunk, the mechanic gave his shoulders a shrug and, in his mobster style, replied:

"Hey, I'm from Brooklyn. In my nay-ba-hood, ya needa gun."

Following Bruce's graduation from Windham in 1974, he turned to a more mundane career as an arborist, apprenticing through jobs with two local tree services until 1979. His father had continued to move, owning two more Manhasset homes through the years, one on Old Pine Drive and the other on Bayview Court.

Scotto found himself in another prime location to collect Manhasset history when he took a seat at Steve Schnitzer's bar - when it was Dickens' and later, Publicans - just around the time JR Moehringer started observing the scenes of his memoir, *The Tender Bar*.

Bruce usually sat in the front and, sometimes, he was asked to check proof for the night, earning $50 and free drinks.

He remembers Chaz McGuire from the days before alapacea took his hair, when Bruce's brother, Tony, first introduced them, and afterwards when Bruce was included in some of those - now legendary - trips to Gilgo Beach with Chaz and crew.

Oh, and Bruce recalls Chaz from the night Bobo of Schnitzer's kitchen crew - "got the crap kicked out of him over by Rocky's gas station," (see *The Tender Bar* for full details).

In 1980, Bruce began his career in telecommunications, and soon after he met Shelley Fleishman of Brooklyn. They married exactly one year later, purchased their first home on Village Road, and in the Scotto tradition, promptly moved into a larger home at 96 Andrew Road when their son, Ian, was born.

Bruce became the commuter dad, Shelley got her real estate license, and Ian grew up playing at the old rock wall on Andrew Road and graduating from the Manhasset public schools.

The town changed here and there as time passed, but it entered a new world at warp-speed on September 11, 2001 and, like all of his neighbors, Bruce saw it happen right before his eyes.

He was at 14 Wall Street in the Banker's Trust Building when the order to evacuate came.

Determined to make his way to Penn Station and home, he joined the crowds of terrorized New Yorkers who now bore the anxiety of knowing a second plane had struck the World Trade Center.

Turning onto Fulton Street, Bruce saw for himself the horror of the raging blaze.

Frantically he tried to call Shelley and couldn't access a local cell signal.

Bruce got through to his brother, Mike, in Pennsylvania. Mike told him about the Pentagon attack and promised to call

Shelley with the news that Bruce was safe and making his way to Manhasset.

Coming up Broadway, news' updates blared from the radios of haphazardly parked cars. A plane had gone down in a Pennsylvania field. Bruce's panic spiked.

He reached LaFayette and Houston to witness thick black smoke pouring from the Trade Center's north tower.

Finally, Shelley answered the phone.

She was with Chris Quackenbush's wife, Tracy.

As Shelley spoke Bruce watched the north tower, where he knew Chris worked, come toppling down "ever-so-slowly" before his eyes.

Scotto stumbled on toward Penn Station with hordes of the stunned and silent - some bandaged and bloodied, others covered in soot.

He thought of the young firefighter he saw hanging on the back of a truck racing toward the towers. He thought of Chris and the many others who had surely died. He thought of getting home to Shelley and Ian.

When he finally reached Midtown, Bruce remembers:

"The most surreal moment came for me. It was like being in some horrific science fiction movie. I looked up and saw four or five fighter jets roaring toward the World Trade Center."

Wounded Long Islanders boarded the first train allowed through the Penn Station tunnels, following a thorough search by the NYPD and bomb-sniffing dogs.

Bruce departed on a later train, and when he stepped off the LIRR in Manhasset, he knew his hometown had changed forever, a fact confirmed with endless weeks of funerals and constantly tolling bells.

The Scottos have taken life a little easier ever since then. These days each works in real estate, and Ian is in the radio business, succeeding at his dream job. They've lived in their Andrew Road home for more than 28 years.

In his spare time, Bruce finds old news' reports or facts about Manhasset icons, and he takes photos of historic Manhasset homes and ancient trees. He posts these on Facebook, offering a few tidbits of history and garnering great discussions from the "I Grew Up in Manhasset..." crowd about Baby Boomer haunts and Gold Coast secrets. He's asked questions about myths and legends and does his best to find the facts when he can.

He's a soft-spoken, storyteller with a gentle laugh when we talk over a table in the front of the legendary bar - where we can't help wondering what ever happened to Publican's famed, stained-glass mural.

Shelley is there and so is my husband. We are four Baby Boomers from Long Island telling stories about the places we have in common. That means, we are laughing and having a great time.

The Scottos say it's not unusual to find them sitting on their patio with friends and family.

Often, they stop to appreciate the chiming carillon of the old Dutch Reformed Church or they pause to remember Chris Quackenbush when they last saw him, standing in the Whitney Boathouse, cigar in hand, pride and joy filling his heart with so many Manhasset stories to tell.

Or Bruce drifts off to his computer, and starts another lively discussion about the year Joan Payson gave Manhasset the Mets or what we'd order if Wetsons suddenly were to appear magically before us.

Moehringer, JR. The Tender Bar. New York: Hyperion, 2005

Obit For A Place:
The Village Bath Club

The vestiges of memory are all that's left once the trees are gone from a familiar place and the asphalt has been laid.

But there is history under every parking lot, a treasure trove of footprints that walked that earth from one dawn to another.

This is just a small part of the story the land from 1900 Northern Boulevard to the stop sign at Mill Spring and Village roads tells, but it's a part that lives vividly in the memory of those who grew up on the streets around The Gate in its early years.

Once it was a land of gracious rolling hills and wooded bliss - sycamores, elms, dogwoods, rhododendrons - with horse trails upon which folks rode before the mid-1930s. Surely residents then were just as upset to see those trees go down, making way for the houses we all treasure so dearly now.

During this time - while the Miracle was becoming a mile long - the area held the Village Bath Club, a discreet, stone-fronted edifice which housed a restaurant adjacent to tennis and pool facilities, while sharing a parking lot with a strip of small businesses.

Among the stores was The Little Brown Shop which filled a quiet corner of the area Apple occupies so boldly now.

It was a place where girls bought the latest volumes of The Bobbsey Twins and Nancy Drew from a kind, older woman who sat at the cramped counter in the back.

The store also sold small, porcelain animals. Little terriers lapping up pails of spilled milk; china cats playing with balls of yarn, baby pigs with muddy snouts. There were shelves of finely wrought, dollhouse furniture and tiny dollhouse families that looked just like ours.

All this and the store smelled like a German bakery, too, because it was next to Frederick's Delicatessen and Tea Room, a small and dearly loved spot where B. Altman shoppers and their daughters often enjoyed plates of the best chicken salad in town.

There was an optometrist's office among the stores where I got my first pair of glasses at age 5 and, in the middle of the strip was the Sunrise Market - about five aisles worth of groceries without automated check out lanes like those at the more modern Food Fair, farther down the boulevard.

Outside Sunrise, deep steps led down to the Strathmore Bowling Alley where a heavy door opened into a dark room with a black bar faced with halved, bowling balls. We had to walk through the bar, our bright eyes adjusting to the cave we'd entered, to get to the lanes in the room beyond where a dollar allowed us to flirt and bowl every winter Saturday.

There was a barber shop on the far end of the stores where I sold my used comic books for two cents a piece and, next to it was Strathmore Drug Store, when pharmacies were called such things, and a man named "Doc" dispensed medicine. It held a long gleaming fountain run expertly by a soda jerk named Mike.

Just across the parking lot was the heart of the area: The Village Bath Club which offered memberships with access to all of its facilities or just to its well-regarded restaurant, run by a maitre d' extraordinaire: Mr. Paul.

The restaurant, like so many of the clubhouses at the time, was a stage for the events of our lives. There, we modeled in fundraising fashion shows, attended celebratory dinners, held afternoon bridal showers and danced at raucous, wedding receptions - my own included.

The pool was alive all summer with the sounds of squealing, splashing kids spending ten hour days there - in the water with crinkly skin, or at the snack bar ordering frozen milky ways, or at the pool's edge perfecting their racing dives for Saturday inter-club meets or Sunday intra-murals.

All day, tennis balls popped back and forth on the clay courts and at night, splash parties with the most popular local bands, attracted teens who never swam, but danced until the 10:30 curfew.

Each year on Labor Day crazy swim events took place at the pool, the last being a greased watermelon race which left the water looking like trash soup when the teenage boys took melons to the high dive and performed stunning cannonballs that produced spectacular explosions of seeds, pulp, and rind.

Consequently the pool was emptied and cleaned promptly the following day, and when it was dry, the caretakers filled the deep end with fresh hay - supposedly to keep us kids from using the cavernous hole as an off-season playground. But the hay just made the pool a more attractive nuisance since word spread quickly after it appeared, and kids from all around the Gates spent a few delightful days jumping into it.

The land became more valuable than the richness the VBC brought to the community and so its demise came slowly through the 80s; houses stand where the tennis courts were and 90 parking spaces outlined on asphalt will provide the stage for a new history - one far less interesting, to be sure - and with fewer trees - and fewer stories to tell.

So this is an obituary for a place and time long gone. May it rest in the peace it once provided as a safe haven for a few generations of kids whose footprints are etched deep in the ground under the blacktop.

~ appeared in the Manhasset Press, August 2012.

Crossing Over to MHS

When we were in high school at St. Mary's, my friends and I met three guys from Manhasset High School who introduced us to a whole new world.

One was Jewish, another was a child of divorce, and the third was of mixed race - normal American types not found among St. Mary's students in the mid-20th century.

These three were the best of friends; the kind of guys with impeccable timing who knew instinctively when to be the straight men and when to score the punch line.

We first met them at the Scratch, aka The Strathmore Hotel, a notorious place on Northern Boulevard where minors with phony birth certificates could be served at the bar.

Yes, the Scratch. It was a total dive - a place that was known as "a beginner's bar." Its hotel was a whore house, if myth be fact.

Let's leave it at this: My mother would have killed me had she known I was there.

In the summer of 1963, the Scratch was transformed into a surfer bar called "The Knotty Knee," with the same lax rules at the door.

Underage kids from Roslyn, Port Washington, East Williston, Manhasset, and beyond jammed the place every weekend.

When my friends and I met our three Manhasset High School wild boys, we were 16 - two years away from drinking legally, so we thought ourselves wild as well.

There were lines around the block that summer, but the bouncer was a guy from Manhasset, so the local girls he knew often got in without queuing up - and without showing any id's whatsoever.

We spotted our three MHS boys as soon as we were ushered ahead to the door upon our first visit to the new place.

They were in the open space behind the bar, dancing to "The Good Rats," a LI band of reknown, still playing today to packed crowds in Long Island bars.

On that night nearly a half century ago, a ring of smiling kids had formed around the Manhasset trio. Wow. Could those guys dance.

The tall boy was lithe and smooth. Black hair, black jeans, blue eyes. He had all the moves. The other two were small and quick - full of music and beer, with their fringe-cut Levi's, bare feet, and 60s teenage magic.

They were doing handsprings and flips, pulling girls from the outer ring into the center, and leading them in the Lindy's of their lives.

Did I mention how cute they were to our virginal 1960s, Catholic school girl eyes?

And before we knew it, each of them had chosen one of us, and there we were - at the center - dancing.

We saw them every weekend that summer, triple dating and cramming into one car.

My guy had longish hair and he'd adopted a Polynesian nickname. It made him sound like a nomad surfer - an image with great appeal at a time when surfing was the new sport of choice among coastal kids.

That's what these guys did all summer - they headed out to Gilgo at 6 a.m. and caught a few waves before going to their summer jobs, then headed back to Gilgo after work to catch a few more.

None of the girls surfed, but the boys preferred us to sit on the sand anyway, watching them catch the curls, wipe out, and stand tall above the sea - again and again.

Afterwards, we went dancing in cheesy LI bars known to avoid checking id's. If we got shot down at the usual dumps, we went to strip clubs.

It's important to say, this knowledge would have made my siblings join my mother in murdering me.

What I remember is: The women weren't very naked by today's stripper standards, and we never stayed very long because it just felt too icky.

I suppose if Billy Joel had already written his song about Catholic girls, "Only the Good Die Young," I would have understood more about the MHS boys' attraction to us that summer - as well ours to them in return. We had crossed into each other's schoolyards when no one was looking, but there were still rules to follow.

I told my surfer boy that he had to come to the door when he picked me up for a date.

I guess he didn't believe me because he pulled into our driveway and honked his horn one night. My older brother, who had inherited the father role when ours died, went charging out of the house to give surfer boy a lesson in etiquette.

The boy got out of the car in his bare feet and took more abuse from my brother before coming into the house to meet my mom who wore a very furrowed brow.

When fall arrived, the guys asked us to a "sock hop" in the MHS gym.

My friends and I were really nervous. I doubt any of us had been in the public high school before that night.

As it turned out, we were invisible anyway.

The band was playing "SHOUT" when we arrived, and our three dancing boys took off for the center of the gym without us - doing their thing just as they had the first night we'd all seen each other at "The Knotty Knee."

They were spectacular, and the kids in the gym - ourselves included - were shouting to the music, throwing our arms up and behaving in conduct deemed "unbecoming" to the St. Mary's students dancing in our gym just a few blocks away.

It was the boys' Senior year at MHS, and we still had two to go at St. Mary's. After that dance, we all went our separate ways.

But I've never forgotten how much fun - and how forbidden - those boys were.

I like to think there's a wee bit of that wild girl left in me, too.

Golf Courses, My Father, and Me

A vista appears before me on my way to a friend's house that startles me every time.

It is the second hole of a Georgia golf course.

I drive through a lush and large neighborhood, following rolling hills and curves toward a crossroad, just to come upon a hillock of varied greens which bursts through a canopy of trees and spreads itself luxuriantly, dead center, before me.

It is a live image that always overwhelms me.

My childhood allowed me to spend time on the golf courses of Long Island's North Shore, and, occasionally, I was actually golfing.

Most times, I was sleigh riding, catching fireflies, roaming roughs for lost balls at sunset, running around in my bare feet on the cool fairways, or waiting in a dripping swimsuit by the kiddie pool for my father to come off the ninth green of Nassau Country Club's course. He'd stop for a damp hug, followed by a quick hello to our mom, and then move on with his foursome.

This was my view, and it is as warm in my memory as it appears on the page.

I now know how fortunate I was. I now know how restricted it was. I now know that exclusion hurts. But then, in the 1950s, I was just young and happy.

That happiness resurrects within me when I see the panorama of a golf course, even though I don't play golf any more.

I did once, but it was a long, long time ago.

My father taught me. He'd found a few second hand, short clubs somewhere, and I'd putt or hit irons at the driving range with him.

Sometimes, he'd take me out to play one or two holes just before the ranger called everyone in. My father would tell me I had a nice swing, and then he'd laugh and say: "Now just put that together with the ball, Susu."

Since I only remember us out there when the sun was going down, the memory is lit with a golden pink backdrop to the undulating whites and greens of the course. My father is wearing peach colored, linen pants with a LaCoste shirt and brown and white golf shoes. Sometimes, he reaches out and hugs me into him.

I played golf with a bit of fervor in my pre-teens, enjoying some nine-hole events here and there in Manhasset - and on random summer eves, a hole or two with my dad at Nassau.

I played at golf in my teens and my 20s, perhaps leading my future husband to believe I cared more than I did.

However I never became a golfer, and yet, rarely does a day of my life pass without the word being mentioned.

I married a man who is a fervent golfer. We have never lived very far from a course, and though it is rare for us to play golf together, I am more conversant about this than any other sport, which has helped sustain us for 40 years.

Golf is the mistress of our marriage, and though there are times when I think she's a time-consuming bitch, most days I love her from afar.

Part of it is because I find golf courses to be irresistible.

In our early years, we loved taking our kids out at dusk to an empty course called Goat Hill. They'd hit at plastic balls and roll down soft green hills while Michael chipped and putted.

The same course called again when the first serious, snow fell each year. We'd all bundle up and head over there to sleigh-ride, finding friends around fires holding ancient wooden toboggans and four-seater, Flexible Flyers, ready to soar down a fairway.

There were other times the water colors of a golf course enchanted us - on visits to tropical islands and a famed course along the Pacific Ocean, oh and once, when we followed the Golden Bear from hole to hole.

The Golf Channel is the fallback station in our house. Golf equipment lines one wall of our garage. There is an annual golf tournament held in my late sister's name. My brother, kids, nephews, in-laws, and oldest friends play golf, and on the rare occasion when I pick up a club to take a shot - again I hear my father's compliment about having a nice swing.

But I remain on the sidelines.

I suppose I know why.

In January 1961, I turned 13 and awoke to a gift from my father staring at me from across the room: a complete set of McGregor clubs in a black, watch plaid bag.

We brought them downstairs and looked at them one by one, sitting on the living room floor. He told me which club performed which task and said, as soon as it got warm enough, we'd go out for nine holes together.

He died before the spring came that year.

It wasn't that I cast the clubs or the game aside, I just never really enjoyed playing it again. So I stopped, and, somehow, never let go.

Then the other day while driving over to my friend's house, I paused when I came to the crest of the hill, taking in the apparition of the fairway, feeling myself fill with the familiar rush that comes, and wondering about the Zen in it.

I can only reason this: For me, on a beautiful golf course at dusk, a real moment exists. I can feel it at will. It's as close as my beating heart, and it's a moment that belongs only to my father and me.

Acknowledgements

Having read of my love for libraries, it will be no surprise to learn that being invited to read from the first book at the Manhasset Public Library in May 2012 was a thrill beyond measure for me.

I am so grateful to the Friends of the Library for hosting the event, and Debbie Dellis-Quinn for managing it so well. Thanks to Maureen Kane Granito for coming from Connecticut and so many others who came from neighboring LI towns.

I am also equally grateful to Debbie Honoroff of Hofstra University's Continuing Education Program for featuring me at a writer's workshop this spring.

Telling more Manhasset stories would never have been possible without an entire village of Manhasset people who have helped.

Among them are Bruce Scotto, Tom Lim, Bob Lubbers, and his daughter, Wendy, who always answered my emails.

Pat Ryan Grace, editor of the Manhasset Press, who featured both the book and its stories in the newspaper.

Mary Ellen Moran Gately and Pat Barnard Kenny, owners of Manhasset's Little Shop around the Corner, who have not only made space for the book in their store, but have also sold it with great enthusiasm and care. The same regards to Dolphin Bookstore in Port Washington.

Special gratitude to Lynn Muller McGrail and her husband, Bob, who graciously opened their Port Washington home to us when we were in New York last spring, and to the Manhasset friends who bought more copies to hand out to other Manhasset friends.

Michele Chisholm Leavitt, MHS grad and textile artist has provided great encouragement, and I'm so grateful. This has led to an invitation to host a writing workshop at her Rhode Island artist's colony. Details are forthcoming!

Thanks to the book clubs who've read the book, to my Mountain Park friends who've listened endlessly to this Yankee talk, to my Manhasset forever friends who've encouraged me to write more stories, and to Joan, Greg and Burnie whose stories are forthcoming.

Thanks to Ingrid Ricks and Laura Novak, writers who help me write.

As for my family, well, my husband Michael has helped keep me together for 40 years, and he's never stopped loving me in the process. Neither have our children, Chris and Mia, who travelled from Atlanta to a reading in New York with Mia's husband Chad. His mom, Judy Kishel, came from Pennsylvania to attend. Thank you, Judy, for that incredible act of kindness. How great that we will soon share a grandchild to love.

Thanks to the McLains and the Smiths because we will always have Manhasset in our DNA, and to the Rosenwassers, Hicksville dwellers, who've put up with my Manhasset stories for decades.

I'm also grateful to JR Moehringer for giving Manhasset *The Tender Bar*. The book may be a great read for others, but for Baby Boomer Manhasset, it's home on paper.

And thanks to my Facebook friends - you know who you are. We've discovered parallel lives loving Weejuns, the same music, and the smell of burning leaves.

To all the Manhasset Baby Boomers and those who love them:

"May you build a ladder to the stars and climb on every rung.
May you stay, forever, young."

~ Bob Dylan

CPSIA information can be obtained at www.ICGtesting.com
Printed in the USA
BVOW041558030413

317202BV00001B/12/P